GHOSTS OF

WAR

The Killing of Captain Wesley Riden

By C. Mark Riden M.A. M.Ed.

Gotham Books
30 N Gould St.
Ste. 20820, Sheridan, WY 82801
https://gothambooksinc.com/

Phone: 1 (307) 464-7800

Published by Gotham Books (July 14, 2022)

ISBN: 978-1-956349-48-1 (sc)
ISBN: 978-1-956349-49-8 (e)

Because of the dynamic nature of the Internet, any web
addresses or links contained in this book may have
changed since publication and may no longer be valid.

Table of Contents

DEDICATION..III

ACKNOWLEDGEMENT V

ABOUT THE AUTHOR VII

IMAGES 2-5

Section1:The Dance of Poets.......................................7

THE UNRETURNING...8

A DEPARTED BROTHER..9

THE BEARDED MEN 10

THE REBEL..11

THE FARMER...12

BLOODIED DRESS BLUES...13

ERSTE MISSIONEN (FIRST MISSIONS)...........................15

BLACK BUTTERFLY: ODE TO THE DEAD.............................16

TECUMSEH'S SPEECH 17

Section 2:The Dance of Ghosts.......................................18

PROLOGUE:Into the Fodder...19

Chapter One:A New Kind of Combat................................29

Chapter Two:Grave Counting...35

Chapter Three:Ghosts of War..49

Chapter Four:Horseshoes and Hand Grenades....................135

Conclusion: Ghosts Be Silent..143

Appendix A: U.S. National Park Service, Department of the Interior 151

Appendix B: Primas Interview..152

Appendix C: The Rolla Fourteen 154

Appendix D: George "Shack" Washington: The Fifteenth Ghost 155

REFERENCE 156

DEDICATION

The first manuscript is dedicated to the 104 United States Marines I recruited and trained during military service, 1979-1994 and 1996-2001.

The book is a gift to my mother, Jessie Fern Hatley Riden who raised me to be strong and overcome the obstacles of life.

The research effort is what I owed to my ancestors of Garrett's, Riden's, Hatley's and Collins,' both living and dead.

ACKNOWLEDGEMENT

I found it inspiring to write salutations with many people, friends, and organizations due of praise. The ghosts of war held special favor and would continue to live in my heart and through these aged hands that scribed their individual stories. Sadly, many ethnographies remained untold or forgotten. Stirred by apparitions of my genetic past, I set out to find the origination of self. Funny that writing a book helped one discover their own existence!

I am extremely appreciative of the citizens who spent time donating information to various second sources. While there seemed to be disagreement among primary and secondary material, the internet proved instrumental in making connections with individual family burial locations as well as military information. Much appreciation was shown to Missouri Digital Heritage genealogists for their extraordinary collections available for online viewing.

A special thank you belonged to writer James Erwin for his expertise on guerilla warfare in Missouri. While stories of Bloody Bill and Jesse James excited the fanatical side of readers, Erwin shared the reality that guerilla fighters and bushwhackers became hunted down and killed for devious acts in reciprocating brutal and inhumane ways. In doing so, Erwin balanced one's perception of the chaos that thundered through the border states during the Civil War.

The essential commodity of writing any book centered on one's access to knowledge. In this life, the ghosts had blessed me with helpful friendly librarians Ann Canavan and Barbara Trombley who kept me stocked with relevant literature and proof sources. Amazingly, while some people may have never picked up a book, these ladies refused to let me put one down.

ABOUT THE AUTHOR

C. Mark Riden is an anthropologist, philosopher, teacher and U.S. military veteran. His alma maters include the University of Central Oklahoma, University of Oklahoma, Rose State College and the United States Marine Corps. In 2014, Riden published The Brain Moves: Traumatic Brain Injury in 21st Century Athletes and Combat Veterans, a research text that evaluates athletic and military-related brain trauma. While in graduate school, Riden served in the university senate representing Student Veterans of America where he wrote and co-sponsored legislation to support military veterans attending college. In 2005, Senator Riden held a seat in the Oklahoma Intercollegiate Legislature.

C. Mark Riden is the great grandson and great nephew of Privates Leonard M. Garrett and John W. Garrett who fought for the Continental Army from 1777-1780 under the command of General George Washington. He is also the grandson of James Riden III, a North Carolina fur trapper who served in the American Revolution at age twelve. Many of the Riden ancestors occupied as captains and privates during the American Civil War. Riden's uncle was Silver Star Recipient Command Sergeant Major Kenneth Merritt, U.S. Army 82nd and 101st Airborne Divisions who served in three theaters of combat, World War II, Korea, and Vietnam.

C. Mark Riden shares ancestry trees with George Washington's sister, New Mexico lawman Pat Garrett, Missouri Sheriff William Herbert Collins, and Cherokee grandmother Susannah Stolen Horse. Riden's roots in Northwest Arkansas are connected to the great pioneer, Wesley Garrett. Summarily, Riden falls into a family tree of explorers and soldiers who migrated westward following the Revolution and the War of 1812.

IMAGES

IMG1: Confederate Guerillas
Source: Kentucky Historical Society & J.B. Martin 1988

IMG2: The Freedom Fighter
Source: Missouri Digital Heritage Collections, 2017

IMG3: James Wesley Riden and Family
Source: K.M. Hoy 2017

IMG4: Cherokee Principal Chief Lewis Downing
Source: Wikimedia Commons, 2022

IMG5: Close combat training with the M16
Source: Marine Corps Recruit Depot San Diego, CA
First Battalion Platoon 1049 Manual, 1980

IMG6: Marksmanship training at San Onofre, CA
Source: Marine Corps Recruit Depot San Diego, CA
First Battalion Platoon 1049 Manual, 1980

IMG7 Pea Ridge Battlefield Artillery
Source: Photograph Courtesy of the Author, Pea
Ridge National Military Park, Arkansas

IMG8: Elkhorn Tavern, Ruddick Home
Source: Photograph Courtesy of the Author, Pea
Ridge National Military Park, Arkansas

SECTION I
The Dance of Poets

THE UNRETURNING

By Wilfred Owen, 1912

*Suddenly night crushed out the day and hurled
her remnants over cloud peaks, thunder-walled.
Then fell a stillness such as harks appalled,
when far-gone dead return upon the World.*

*There watched I for the dead, but no ghost woke.
Each one whom life exiled I named and called.
But they were all too far, or dumbed, or thralled,
and never one fared back to me or spoke.*

*Then peered the indefinite unshapen dawn.
With vacant gloaming, sad as half-lit minds,
the weak-limned hour when sick men's sighs are drained.*

*And while I wondered on their being withdrawn,
gagged by the smothering wing which none unbinds,
I dreaded even a Heaven with doors so chained.*

A DEPARTED BROTHER

By L.B. Flanders, 1863

I thought he came at dewy eve,
to whisper in my ear,
but now I know in morn's pale beam,
my brother lost, is near.
I know him by the gentle rap
upon the inner door,
of my sad heart, so like the rap
he used to give of yore.
I know him by the gentle words:
'Awake! My sister dear;'
so like the gentle words of old,
my ear was wont to hear.
And, too, my soul discerns the smile
that lights his pleasant eye;
so like the smile it used to wear
ere he ascended high.
And the blest counsels that he breathes,
I heed with willing ear,
for well I know where wisdom reigns,
there reigns my brother dear.

THE BEARDED MEN

By C. Mark Riden, 2016

The bearded men lead their ghost platoons,
With marching orders in hand,
To steal the day and promise to pay
The debts of war demand.

Battlefields lined with corpses of brothers.
What shall we tell the wives and mothers?
Sisters weep and scowl,
The dogs of darkness howl.

Distemper in the backbone of boyhood fraught,
Explicated by the spoils of untimely begot.
The bearded men shadowed by private fires,
Scatter their secrets in the funeral pyre.

In the horror of deeds, lowly privates none the wiser,
Bleeding and dying by the confinement of slaughter.
Colonels commanding and the captains praised,
Lieutenants confused, let the flag be raised.

Drowned by the thunder of howitzer plunder,
Let no Yankee put asunder, we cried.
Let no Yankee put asunder.

The bearded men dawn metals on sleeves,
provoking the habits of mad men and thieves.
And who are we to consider such plight?
But killers ourselves in this Civil War fight.

THE REBEL

By C. Mark Riden, 2017

*Comfortably numbed by riches and furs, rambling wishes
and slurs, uninvited tokens of the blurred, the storm of
rebellion reassured.*

*Treaties crafted by thoughtless buzzards and gutless men,
Lives broken and tattered, smothered and battered, patented
and lathered.*

*Truth and honor claimed no victory to the ravaged and
enraged.*

*Courage and bravery served no model for the mortified and
disengaged.*

*Laws the Northerners had made fore they would soon bend.
Debts of disobedience would determine our unholy sin.
Lincoln consumed the cake Jefferson baked but then
bartered by mistake.*

*When we failed to provide hook, the Union generals forcibly
took.*

*It's okay to be them, but not right to be us, and discuss
what must be just.*

*The books they wrote, they suddenly and spitefully
changed.*

*It became hard to keep pace with the invalid and strange.
Mostly there's a Heaven but sometimes cometh the hell.
Clearly, we had no choice but to rebel.*

THE FARMER

By Amelia E. Barr, 1836

The king may rule o'er land and sea,
The lord may live right royally,
The soldier rides in pomp and pride,
The sailor roam o'er ocean wide;
But this or that, whate'er befall,
The farmer he must feed them all.

The writer thinks, the poet sings,
The craftsmen fashion wondrous things,
The doctor heals, the lawyer pleads,
The miner follows the precious leads;
But this or that, whate'er befall,
The farmer he must feed them all.

The merchant he may buy and sell,
The teacher do his duty well;
But men may toil through busy days,
Or men may stroll through pleasant ways;
From king to beggar, whate'er befall,
The farmer he must feed them all.

The farmer's trade is one of worth;
He's partner with the sky and Earth,
He's partner with the sun and rain,
And no man loses for his gain;
And men may rise, or men may fall,
But the farmer he must feed them all.

God bless the man who sows the wheat,
Who finds us milk and fruit and meat;
May his purse be heavy, his heart be light,
His cattle and corn and all go right;
God bless the seeds his hands let fall,
For the farmer he must feed us all.

BLOODIED DRESS BLUES

By Gunnery Sergeant C. M. Riden, 1996

You were my brothers; we were born America's sons.
On the day that you died, Lord knows the good died young.
Your final orders came one deadly April day,
They covered you in a tattered flag, and then carried you
away.

Because ceilings fell and the concrete crumbled,
Children scurried, little Baylee stumbled,
Dust flew like bullets, and bricks fell like bombs,
Awakened by the morning news,
Tattoos and patent leather shoes,
Blood stripes and bloodied dress blues.

I heard the mother's crying, with hearts so full of emotion,
Their tears streaming down like rivers flowing toward the
ocean,
Never thought they'd being saying goodbye on that deadly
April day,
They covered you in a tattered flag, and then carried you
away.

Because ceilings fell, and the concrete crumbled
Children scurried, little Baylee stumbled,
Dust flew like bullets, and bricks fell like bombs,
Awakened by the morning news,
Tattoos and patent leather shoes,
Blood stripes and bloodied dress blues.

We were too young to serve in Vietnam,
But today Oklahoma fell like Saigon,
Taps played so beautiful on that deadly April day,
I said my Semper Fi's
I told one last sea story lie…

13

*They covered you in a tattered flag, and then carried you
away.*

*Because ceilings fell, and the concrete crumbled
Children scurried, little Baylee stumbled,
Dust flew like bullets, and bricks fells like bombs,
Awakened by the morning news,
Tattoos and patent leather shoes,
Blood stripes and bloodied dress blues.*

I should have died with you.

By C. Mark Riden, 2007

We move through the warming water, silently, quietly drifting with ease, drawn into the bowels of Hades like messengers of twisted wrath. Our hearts empty of forgiveness and full of contempt, desperately, defiantly in need of treasures and skulls, we creep to the river's edge. Accompanied by the battle-axe, let our journey fulfill the morbidities of our fathers and brothers. As I give the order with silent hand, the men slither over the sides of the longship like leeches in dire straits for blood. We will rape the land for its sources, pillage that which Odin commands, burn down the houses of the holy, and feast upon the bones of the righteous. We offer no quarter in return. As we begin our advance, I whisper to myself, 'Oh great God of War, bless these poor farmers.'

Inaudible but violent, we move with stealth peeping, creeping, crawling like ticks on a deer into the kill zone at which time I command the men to take cover in the tall typha grass. Momentarily delayed, we hunker down in wait for recon team two to make its way to the rendezvous point. Caged beasts ready to devour, the men salivate like wolves thirsty for the slaughter of lambs. Impatiently, I see the shadows of team two fill the beachhead and insurge with precision. In columns, we maneuver the teams onto the dirt road leading to the Lindisfarne Monastery and force-march to the contact point, shields up, steel extended, ears open, eyes focused.

By C. Mark Riden, 2008, 2020

The black butterfly tizzies only at night.
Fly butterfly fly.
Fly higher and higher into the dark sky.
We see you can fly, fluttering by and by, then by and by.
Like an eagle soaring, reaching for the blind wind,
which it cannot see or touch but feel.
So cool and warm rages midnight breezes,
so cold and hot Earth does as it pleases.
Fly butterfly fly.
Beautiful is your flight, graceful gliding into the blackened
night.
Others abstain to move at such plight.
The black butterfly flaps only alone, climbing then diving
abounded.
Fly butterfly fly.
Fly longer and longer and farther, farther still farther.
We see you can fly, descrying smaller objects on the
ground.
Stretched wings delicate to the touch but strong against the
wind.
Fly butterfly fly.
Intoxicating by your gazes, with twists and turns and
airborne phrases.
And as you drift back down,
you aspire to the ground like a dandelion seed floating,
floating gently to its final resting spot.
Fly butterfly fly.
Fly higher into the midnight sky.
Feel the clamor on your cotton wing,
passing glances to the birds as they sing.
Unusual fancied wonderment forever reaching to Heaven.
Fly butterfly fly.

TECUMSEH'S SPEECH

Spoken near the Tombigbee River, Mississippi, 1811

We meet tonight in solemn council not to debate whether we have been wronged or injured, but to decide how to avenge ourselves. Have we not courage enough to defend our country and maintain our ancient independence? Where today are the Pequot? Where are the Narragansett, the Mohawk, the Pocanet and the powerful tribes of our people? They have vanished before the avarice and oppression of the white man, as snow before the summer sun... So it will be with you! Soon your mighty forest trees will be cut down to fence-in the land. Soon their broad roads will pass over the graves of your fathers. You too will be driven from your native land as leaves are driven before the winter storm...

SECTION II
The Dance of Ghosts

Into the Fodder

Francisco Pizzaro conquered the great Inca leader Atahualpa in 1532. By 1736, tribes like the Timucua had vanished. Chief Tecumseh's message too would one day become actuality. He died in the Battle of Thames, 1813. The European conquest of the Americas moved forward, our lands forcibly appropriated, with weapons drawn and diseases packaged.

It seemed impossible to have calculated with specificity how much had been lost in war. America looked to always become betrothed to some degree by armed conflict. Inevitably, we tended to kill ourselves more often than we killed our enemies. The ghosts of war clamored to be heard so I opened the door. "We live, we die, and death not ends it" wrote Jim Morrison in An American Prayer. Tecumseh's passing did not end a warrior's struggle but instead tethered its survival.

I enjoyed writing about topics that stowed away in the ships of humankind, especially those with a dark military invocation. There existed no shame in serving one's country of course. Admittedly prone to infer and philosophize, in this book I wanted to highlight stories of citizens and veterans immersed in war that anthropologists and historians had overlooked, failed to see credibility in, or were too nervous or ashamed to bring up. The only way to find truth appeared distinctly obvious: I needed to extenuate the darkness. So, like a mad man, into the fodder I went.

We all had obscurities that needed to be tamed. I started and concluded the research for this book in a graveyard. In the Ghosts of War, using grave markers as stepping stones into the past, I tackled the momentous job of retrieving information pertaining to individual military service and genealogy centered on a base of frontiersmen and civil conflict. Critics of my first book had remarked that at times I lacked centrality and focus. While it may have been true that I teetered on the strange and abstract, there existed no way to feather men killing and dying in grotesque ways, especially when they originated from one's own family tree. As the American Civil War found its way onto the Great Plains, citizen-soldiers responded and took up arms (See The Rebel; see also IMG1). Against a superior force, we converted into guerillas.

> If you look at your reflection at the bottom of the well, what you see is only on the surface. When you try to see the meaning hidden underneath, the measure of the depth can be deceiving. The bottom has a rocky reputation (Joe Walsh, The Confessor, 1985).

Over and over again in this book, I gravitated toward unique interesting particulars about military veterans' lives and the dispositions of their nuclear and extended families. Along the way, I met wonderful people of culture, viewed beautiful landscapes, and investigated the remarkable lives of the dead. Holistically, it became directly evident to me that the courageous Cherokee and other ethnic groups cascaded by war had indeed survived and faced difficult times to come westward, either through emigration or forced removal. These families became the first true pioneers of the West. My genetic line of descent appeared in the middle of it all.

In writing this book, I hoped to tease readers with the idea that our ancestors had been connected to us in more ways than we recognized, especially spiritually, but also socially, politically and even militarily. Our failure as mortals and descendants to look inward toward the creation of "us" had caused the ghosts of war to become restless. After fighting in combat, the ghosts turned to building a country.

With respect to sources in the book, historical recount had changed significantly where information in the current century had been digitized and made accessible from hand-written archives. Computer technology had spurned a flood of reworked knowledge, some of which appeared useable, while other pieces not so much. Missing information as well as names being misspelled remained problematic. In some cases, material could not be corroborated because of a lack of attention to detail. To complicate matters, genealogical mistakes could be found in most of the websites that charged a fee for discovery.

On point, I had never condoned electronic industries trading away for profit a person's good name or heritage. Try to order a publicly-owned death certificate on one of your relatives and you will get blocked by commercial outlets literally selling your own history back to you. What would cost you $5 at your local state office would cost you $159.95 and a contractual obligation with a corporation. Businesses had been vending your family records for huge revenue. Had you been paid any royalties? Luckily, I was able to work around most of the nonsense because of my education and research experience. One of the biggest disappointments of the research turned out to be a lack of credible photographic evidence on individual family members and combat units.

Ancestral research revealed itself to be a hot topic in the last ten years. Everyone inside academia seemed to be getting on board. In search of originality, I had to dig deep like a social archaeologist sifting through layers of time. I expected to find that missing in modern historical conjecture had been talented and creative ghosts of war living beyond their own earthly existence but unknown, hardly mentioned, or plainly forgotten. As a scholar, it seemed disturbing to think that what mankind professed to know of sociocultural anthropology was not that much at all. Some ghosts had been left out of the conversation for more than one-hundred and fifty years.

Valid and reliable research always seemed to stumble on the inexcusable. This book had its moments for sure. Exploratory work presented evidence that struck at the core of the investigative effort. During the inquiries for this book, I discovered the gruesome Riden murders of 1864. The deaths brought new meaning to the word "family."

Although less tragic, I found out that the Riden's had a cave in Missouri which now stood as a bat sanctuary. Thus far, I had been denied access to it. Geographical investigations at the turn of the twentieth century had noted the grid location of an extravagant cave system in Southwest Missouri and specifically Riden's Cave near Big Piney, close to the property of my great uncle, Captain (John) Wesley Riden (1818-1864). Once the temporary lodging of early Native Americans, during the Civil War, guerilla units often used the Ozark caves to avoid being seen by federal scouting parties.

Words brought people together but also drove them apart. There could be no in-between. The result was civil conflict and savagery on the eastern edge of the Great Plains. The search for myths and truths proved to be something we could all share in common. The initial wave of frontier families that arrived on the Plains in the early 1800s farmed, mined, raised children, and prayed for rain. Indian Nations and whites brought slaves with them onto the prairie. Dominantly, early settlers practiced Christianity, which for me seemed rather odd and ethnocentric given the fact that they maintained human beings against their will.

As personified in Bryan and Rose's (1876) treatise, "pioneers were not lawless people" (p. 89). They became leaders in their communities and entrenched themselves in forming governments and establishing laws. First families appeared highly organized, resourceful, ruled and structurally involved in town-building. Political work focused on establishing county seats, schools and land appropriation. Documents drawn and papers entrusted, pioneers held elections and debated over who should represent their interests.

Early pioneers were tough people who possessed an undefinable strength of character. To think of the families as backward and uneducated would have been carelessly contrived. Settlers proved to be incredibly loyal, determined, and smart. Children grew up fast. Destined to become farmers, the early Plains settlers became the great agriculturalists of the West (See The Farmer). Garrett's and Riden's were among the first families to till Missouri soil.

The Garrett-Riden genetic tree and its extensions had been recorded as two of the original settler families that emigrated to Missouri in 1817 following the American Revolution and the War of 1812. Among the pool of ghosts, my fifth-generation great grandfather and uncle presented in this book (Chapter 3) had served in the Third Maryland Infantry Regiment from February 1777 to February 1780 and could be found listed on the official Valley Forge Muster Rolls. Aided by the help of his Riden son-in-law, Grandfather Leonard M. Garrett (1759-1826) used his worldly experiences to move the entire Garrett-Riden family from South Carolina into Missouri by mules, wagons, and the Mississippi River.

While in South Carolina, the Garrett's and Riden's lived in the lands of the Cherokee. Ironically, my maternal grandparents Sam and Alma Hatley of Stilwell, Oklahoma had raised their children in the old Cherokee Goingsnake District in Eastern Oklahoma at Oak Grove. On a map, the Oak Grove community looked to be about 14.9 miles from Westville, Oklahoma where the Trail of Tears officially ended. When I grew up, the Cherokee Nation elected Wilma Mankiller (1945-2010) as Principal Chief. The Cherokee Nation and its people have continually remained a big part of our family.

Several of my full and half cousins shared a Cherokee bloodline. An uncle carried the surname Walkingstick. My own father's mother hid her Native heritage for most of her life, even from her own grandson. Grandfather William Charles Riden from Rolla, Missouri married a woman of Cherokee descent.

While at college, I studied the Cheyenne and Sioux. Melvin Tall Bull and Robert Horse became my friends in childhood. Robert shared a mixed gene pool with the Kiowa and the Chickasaw. Melvin had been related to the great Cheyenne Chief Tall Bull killed at the Battle of Summit Springs, Colorado. I enjoyed the readings on the Paiute religious leader Wovoka and Sioux medicine man Tatanka Yotanka also known as Sitting Bull. In the 1960s, my mother took me to the Pow Wows in Anadarko, Oklahoma with her good friend, Ruby Horse.

During my formal academic years, I studied Native American History and Ritual where I developed a disrespect for the Osage and Crow who scouted for the American cavalry under fouled leaders George Armstrong Custer and John Chivington, officers known to attack and kill women and children. In 1998, I toured the Ouachita Battlefield where Chief Black Kettle and his wife had been slain. Later in 2014, while marketing The Brain Moves in Colorado, I viewed the battlefield at Sand Creek where Black Kettle had been seen flying the American flag outside his lodge pole shortly before being attacked. Studying the plight of the various Indian Nations has helped me understand what it would have been like to be conquered. I could now speak with indemnity on how it truly felt to be "rubbed out."

In a family, uncles had a special role. For young boys, uncles proved to have a similar function like dads. The process of manhood was keenly vested in the impressions made by uncle to nephew. Uncle Louis B. Lackey had served fighting off Japanese aircraft in World War II as part of the Army-Air Corps. Born on the same day in December, I learned how to drive fast from "Uncle Lucky."

All of my first-generation uncle's served in the U.S. military: Uncle Melferd Kulp fought Hitler and the Germans riding a motorcycle. Uncle Kenneth Merritt received the Silver Star for his jump into Normandy during Operation Overlord. In 2014, he was awarded France's highest medal and taken for a ride aboard Marine One. Uncle Leonard Mc Main was on his way to Okinawa when the atomic bomb was dropped on Hiroshima in 1945. Uncle Phil Riden had served on submarines in the Navy.

During the Cold War, Uncle Bob Riemer maintained an Air Force post in Germany near Berlin with a top-secret clearance. Uncle Calvin "Cap" Walkingstick had served in the Army as a field cook. Uncle Jim Hatley completed an airman's tour and Uncle Ole Hatley, the family preacher, spent time on Guam.

The prevailing theme of my uncle's had been service, sacrifice, and loyalty to country. In 1861, when the Yankees invaded Riden land in Missouri, I could be certain my ancestors who had honorably involved themselves in the law and defense of America felt slighted if not down-right disrespected. The Republic they had once safeguarded now turned-coat. There existed little doubt in my mind that Captain Wesley Riden's arrests had been based on his reaction to being distastefully invaded by the Federals.

To my knowledge, my family never involved itself in the preposterous and ugly trading of humans. Grandfather Garrett had two male slaves listed on a U.S. Census Report living with him in South Carolina. Conversely, they dropped off later census reports after his death. Files showed that the slaves may have been inherited and lived with Elizabeth Garrett Riden (1793-1852), his daughter and my great grandmother, until about 1835.

Elizabeth detested slavery because after her death, during her husband's second marriage, only an elderly African woman could be identified living with Joseph Sr. I found confidence in the thought that Grandma Elizabeth gave Leonard's two slaves freedom long before the start of the Civil War.

As the Garrett-Riden brood expanded, farm labor became no longer needed. The Riden families established property in five Missouri counties: Pulaski, Phelps, Shannon, Saint Francois, and Texas County. One might expect to find the use of slaves with so much land to maintain but the archives discounted such discovery. By the time war found its way onto the Plains, the Garrett's and Riden's had already lived in Missouri and Arkansas forty years.

In a system that degraded people killing-off future generations, it was only a matter of time when the abomination of slavery would pit its creators against its abolitionists. Ultimately, a monster would try to digest its own bowel! The Steven Douglass Bill called the Kansas and Nebraska Act 1854 usurped the Missouri Compromise and changed the Mason-Dixon Line. In an effort to build the Transcontinental Railroad through the Great Plains, Douglas' legislation ended up drawing battle lines between pro and anti-slavers over popular sovereignty. The Douglas document divided the Nebraska Territory into Kansas and Nebraska.

Division and animosity in Kansas led to political violence in Washington D.C. In the U.S. Congress, Senator Charles Sumner of Massachusetts was beaten unconscious by Preston Brooks from South Carolina after Sumner's denunciation of "the crime against Kansas" (Foner, 2006, p. 422). Like moths to a flame, settlers flocked to Kansas in droves. The clash, stimulated by the voting proposition over popular sovereignty, turned deadly. Bleeding Kansas became the major precursor to total war.

Trepidations for new settlers living in the Midwest and especially in Kansas Territory worried the executive department. President James Buchanan's Administration grew concerned over tensions related to the issue of "extending slavery into the western territories" (Stewart, 2008, p. 197). Fierce fighting on the Kansas-Missouri border between the Jayhawkers and the Ruffians ushered in a new breed of warfighters, the bushwhacker and guerilla. The nastiest of characters, William Quantrill once said:

> The hanging of John Brown had been too good for him and that the devil had got unlimited sway over this territory, and will hold it [he would] until we have a better set of man and society generally (Connelley, 1956, p. 94-96).

When the Union Army finally landed in Missouri in 1861, hell-fire and damnation tagged along. One might have claimed that Josey Whales had just walked through the front door. Ulysses S. Grant and his general officers had not planned on fighting farmers or the Indian Nations to the degree that eventually played out on the battlefields and in the forests of the Great Plains. Underestimating the opposition while lacking a clear understanding of the area, Union forces became frequently overwhelmed by superior tactics. Misfortune in Missouri meant trouble in the remaining border states for pioneer families.

The Union officers and enlisted personnel who were sent for duty in the territories and border states during the Civil War had no fathom of what they would be up against. They were outsiders and did not know how to fight in a jungle. Commonly, U.S. Army soldiers understood the phalanx, single envelopment, and flanking maneuver but had very little training on how to exploit elevation or uplifted terrain and knew nothing about the art of camouflage, things my Native brothers had practiced for thousands of years.

Civil unrest confused agriculturalists. Many had been military veterans who had used their Bounty Land Warrants to start a new life. Farmers did not understand why their property had been occupied. Families, friends and neighbors turned on each other over the peculiar institution of slavery, the political question of state sovereignty, and the rights and wrongs of an invading federal army. Farms burned and trains bombed, kinship and genetic heritage became severed forever by war and lawlessness.

Many courageous soldiers who had answered the call to arms became maimed, killed, captured or imprisoned by war. A new kind of combat came to town in Arkansas, Kansas, Missouri and Oklahoma.

CHAPTER ONE

A New Kind of Combat

There existed two kinds of combat: One with laws, the other with force. The first was proper to man, the second to beasts, but because the first was often not enough, one must have recourse to the second (Minter, 1992; Mansfield trans. 1985).

America's appetite for combat first developed in the Revolution followed by the battles against Tecumseh, the War of 1812, the Red Stick War, the First Seminole War, the Black Hawk War, and the Mexican-American War. An experienced fleet of Union and Confederate platoon leaders had been formally educated at West Point and The Citadel which gave their war departments an unprecedented military advantage. By the end of the Civil War, the style of combat in the Trans-Mississippi gave the act of battling new meaning.

Kensey (2002) recognized the fact that West Point students only received training in Napoleonic Principles (p. 4). When their boots hit ground in Missouri, leaders appeared befuddled by paramilitary activity. Tactical aspects of combat differed from conflict to conflict because of changes in the environment, terrain, and force-size. It was hard to shoot what you could not see! This became something American combat forces would relearn later in Vietnam.

With its grandiose flora and fauna, the border states and western territories looked well-suited to provide food, cover and camouflage to nomadic guerilla fighters and bushwhackers. The extensive cave system of the Ozarks offered superfluous advantages for short and long-range reconnaissance. Farmers turned to soldiering as a way to safeguard their families, farms and futures. Some became outlaws and murderers while others took to bombing bridges and trains. Fragmented and desperate for change, Missouri became the carbon copy of a state riddled with freedom fighting (Parrish, 1965; also see IMG2).

When a plot to blow up the Gasconade Train surfaced, Riden family members died at the hands of Union soldiers. In as much, I had no choice but to reposition myself inside the fodder. I invested in both of Erwin's (2012, 2013) work covering guerillas and guerilla hunters of the Civil War hoping to find particulars on my great uncle, Captain Wesley Riden. According to Erwin (2013), the burden of guerilla hunting fell on the Missouri State Militia Cavalry (p. 34). According to eyewitness testimony, a scoundrel cavalry unit had killed the Riden's.

Nichols (2014) recognized that in the fall of 1861, thousands of southern recruits riding to Southwest Missouri to join the Rebel cause "carried out numerous acts of sabotage against the railroad infrastructure operated by Union forces" resulting in train derailments and innocent civilians being killed or injured (p. 7). As their enemy continued to encroach, Rebels started setting fire to and blowing up trains and bridges to halt their advance. The telegraph line became an important target for fighters because they could cut off vital communications between Union commanders in the field.

What looked to be a new kind of combat for Easterners and Europeans seemed to be old hat for the Cherokee of Oklahoma Indian Territory. The Cherokee knew how to fight bush warfare and implement covert techniques. They never wanted to be farmers in the first place! Following removal, the Nation divided over the signing of the Treaty of New Echota. Internally, the Cherokee started bushwhacking each other.

In 1839, treaty signers Major Ridge, John Ridge and Elias Boudinot were stabbed to death by unknown assailants (Cassidy et al., 1995, p. 75). Little did the Cherokee realize at the time of the

Civil War that by 1890, the Curtis Act would effectively "abolish their tribal governments" and "cut them off from the statehood process" (Cassidy et al., 1995, p. 347).

Records covering the beginning days of the Civil War spoke of its immediate effect on Oklahoma Indians. The new war put pressure on Chief Stand Watie (De-ga-ta-ga) and the Cherokee to defeat an overwhelming monstrosity of Union cavalry in the hills of Eastern Oklahoma. Confederate units quickly formed and went on the offensive. Led by Watie, the Cherokee joined the fight naturally siding with the Confederacy. Those of Cherokee descent who chose to fight on the side of the Union would be regarded as traitors.

> That country never bleeds in vain, when the dread curse of war falls on her. Though with a hecatomb of slain, she vindicates insulted honor. When kind paternal words are weak, and spurned the calm appeal of reason. The cannon's iron lips must speak, in thunder to the brood of treason. (W.H.C. Hosmer, 1873, p. 63-64)

The Cherokee ghosts of war that I personally knew of because of family ties had all been buried in the Oak Grove Cemetery, Chalk Bluff Cemetery, or Piney Cemetery in and near Stilwell, Oklahoma. Remembrances of the noble warrior would not be forgotten in my lifetime:

> Long in tooth and soul. Longing for another win. Lurch into the fray, weapon out and belly in. Warrior struggling to remain consequential. Bellow aloud, bold and proud of where I've been. But here I am…beating chest and drums! (Tool, Invincible, 2019).

For hundreds of years, the U.S. Government had punched Native Americans in the Ee-koo-pee, the Lakota Sioux word for "stomach" (Hyeriand Starijing, 1866). Civil War in Indian Territory offered a chance for payback, qualified blood reparations if you will. In the Indian Nations, Cherokee combatants held the upper hand.

The ruthless nature of combat that consumed states Arkansas, Kansas, Missouri and Oklahoma became something President Lincoln's Secretary of War Edwin Stanton could never have anticipated. Clearly, he underestimated Stand Watie. Fighting on an open plane was one strategy, but not a wise one. Fighting in a woodland environment presented new and unexpected challenges. With the stakes higher, the killing turned exceptionally vicious. Body mutilation proved to be common which included scalping and the taking of ears.

Confederate soldiers drew on joint alliances with their Cherokee partners, a relationship first established from living with each other in the Smoky Mountains of North Carolina and Tennessee. Cherokee and Confederate soldiers understood their surroundings. The Civil War became the first time in history that the Cherokee had the chance to finally win a conflict using a significant proportion of their white friends against their white enemies. Cherokee warriors dressed in Confederate blue and gray served honorably by training young privates in the art of stealth and ambush.

Being that the two allied in trade, the Cherokee had fought on the side of the British in the American Revolution. However, the Cherokee had refused to fight in the War of 1812 with their neighbors, the Creeks, against Major General Andrew Jackson. In the Civil War, the Cherokee had few choices. Thirty-four years after forced removal, had the Cherokee Nation suddenly found motivation to forgive a government that had caused the deaths of thousands of its people? I thought not. The political constructs of broken treaties and cracked promises played out in hostile ways. War divided loyalties and thus divided the Indian Nations further.

Certainly, some Cherokee fought with Union forces in a skirmish line and held special duty assignments. Selected fighters who served in units with white Confederates became horse-mounted guerillas. Born to lead, General Watie was the last Confederate officer to surrender in 1865 (Davis, 1999). The astute field commander had been found buried with honor in the Polson Cemetery in Delaware County, Oklahoma.

When the Civil War ended, the Federals had not suffocated the guerillas nor had they succeeded at stopping bushwhacking. Ewing (2013) disagreed emphasizing that thousands of Union hunters had killed off the troublesome guerillas loyal to the Confederacy. Missouri guerillas that had been captured faced sure death, either to be immediately twisted by the noose or imprisoned in St. Louis at the Gratiot Street and Myrtle Street Prisons or across the Mississippi River in Alton, Illinois. It seemed best to die in battle than inside a disease-ridden custodial. Unfortunately, these kinds of graves could never be counted accurately.

CHAPTER TWO

Grave Counting

Featured at the Sam Noble Museum on the campus of my alma mater, a marble engraving read: "The Face of Earth is a Graveyard." The bodies of our dead ancestors held special favor in our historical heritage. The idea of researching history from the grave seemed to be a candid way of paying respect, even if it appeared a bit dark in methodology. Honestly, I appreciated the fact that people found my yearnings somewhat strange.

The expression "grave counting" evolved into a manner of uncovering my own cultural history as I learned about so many others. De Jean had written "that gravestone markers revealed information about the movement of people and often provided evidence of previous cultural ties" (2012, p. 3). I soon gained an appreciation for De Jean's remarks in my travels into Arkansas and Oklahoma. The drive from Springdale to Alma, Arkansas through the Ozark National Forest proved to be spectacular.

Missouri became an official part of the United States in 1821. Arkansas established statehood fifteen years later in 1836. Kansas received inclusion in 1861 when the Civil War began. Oklahoma did not attain statehood until 1907 following five land-runs. The various cemeteries that were explored and the gravesites that were analyzed confirmed my intuitions: I found a pronounced connection to the old country of the Eastern Frontier, burial sites that had been established by early pioneer families, generations that had been directly affected by war, and two murders if not three.

New states and territories became riddled with cultural, social, economic and political anarchy throughout the 1850s and 1860s. Lawrence, KS had been burned. The Cherokee had become entwined in political civil war. Bushwhackers like William Quantrill and Bill Anderson killed and plundered in excess. Somewhere in the madness rode Jesse and Frank James. It became a period where the attributes of Americans as rugged individuals would be pressed to the limit to say the least. Citizens and soldiers battled over unfair treaties, the atrocity of slavery, the rights of property, political leadership, and military insurrection. People maimed and exterminated one another by unimaginable means.

Nineteenth-century cemetery plots and graves communicated a time in human existence where society, while genuinely caring and good-natured, wavered on destruction. Many a soldier found his place in the dirt. The social upheaval that hit the Great Plains like a tornado pushed people to preaching and praying, soldiering, outlawing, bushwhacking, and guerilla-fighting. Life in Missouri would not begin to settle until the end of the Civil War. Hard times still lay ahead for the Cherokee of Indian Territory after 1865.

Rolla, Missouri eventually became my research base. I crossed the state line into Western Missouri in the summer, 2016. Rolla was centrally located and within a stone's throw of St. Louis one-hundred miles away. Rumored to be named for a good-for-nothing hunting dog, early in the Civil War, Rolla became a district controlled by the Federals. Wild Bill Hickok (1837-1876) worked for the Provost Marshal in Rolla in 1864 when Captain Wesley Riden was killed. Did I believe he knew of Wesley's rebellious ways? The answer could only be an angry 'absolutely!'

Guerilla warfare seemed to be the only real agreeable response Missouri farmers could make against a large invading force trampling on popular sovereignty. The Federals were trespassing on farmland owned by war veterans. Imprisonment and severe punishment for entertaining Confederate sympathies never took but only enraged people further. Pushed off their property, the farmer-turned-fighter died where they fell away from home and family. Anonymous burial meant one could be misplaced but never forgotten.

War became especially hard on kinfolk hoping to reunite with their loved one's body. Union dead needed to be shipped home which was not always possible. The Civil War created a numerical and logistical nightmare to say the least. A soldier's burial depended on the total number of casualties in a specific battle. Take Gettysburg, for instance: after the fighting, because fatality numbers were so high for both sides, shallow mass committal had to be utilized. The bodies of the dead had become bloated and diseased causing a health risk.

Without a formal system of identification such as dog tags, burial identification was not completely feasible. Dog tags did not come into existence until 1913 when they were mandatory. In 1862, the Federals started establishing national cemeteries. Arlington National Cemetery was built on General Robert E. Lee's property. Coming up with authenticated Confederate burial sites proved to be a momentous task by comparison. I began to believe that many of the Rebel-marked graves had been unoccupied.

Pioneering families wanted to live near where they buried their dead ancestors. Federal invasion coupled with sheer savagery disrupted the natural order of things. Union soldiers proved to be as horrific as their Confederate counterparts when it came to not only killing but dismembering opponents. This fact made body accountability practically impossible.

A strange burial case appeared regarding the physical remains of legendary Confederate guerilla raider, William Quantrill. After he died, the body was immediately buried in Louisville, Kentucky close to where he had fought. In a disingenuous manner twenty years later, his bones were unearthed and the skull used in a fraternity ritual until 1942 (Brooks, 2013). Incredibly, Quantrill's bones eventually changed hands more than five times.

According to Brooks (2013), some of Quantrill's bones became the property of the Kansas State Historical Society; his skull found its final resting place on the Quantrill Family Plot in the Fourth Street Cemetery in Dover, Ohio; and his arm and a shinbone were buried in the Old Confederate Veteran's Home Cemetery in Higginsville, Missouri.

The Rolla and Watts Cemeteries held the remains of the largest population of surnamed Riden family members in Missouri. The Watts Cemetery in Pulaski County had 13 Riden-named graves. The Rolla Cemetery in Phelps County looked huge with a total of 6,421 graves, 18 of which belonged to a Riden. The Burnett Cemetery in Texas County at Licking and the Beaver Cemetery in Phelps County had only 5 Riden graves. The Burnett Cemetery had also been called the Piney River Cemetery.

In the State of Missouri alone, there appeared a total of 57 Riden burials, the majority of which were clustered in Pulaski and Phelps Counties. Naturally, these numbers did not account for genetic drift in successive family-tied generations. For example, Great Aunt Nancy Garrett Dent had been buried with the Dent family because of her marriage to Mark Dent, father of Lewis Dent whose name bore the county designation in Arkansas.

Based on the earliest dates and places of birth of Riden descendants now buried across the Great Plains, evidence showed that the Riden family tree had been continued through my great grandmother's marriage to Joseph Warren Riden Sr. (1797-1896), a South Carolinian with mixed Cherokee blood.

Elizabeth and Joseph's birthdates were the earliest on record, both interred at the Burnett Cemetery in Licking, Missouri and not at Rolla. Federal documents showed that Joseph and Elizabeth married in South Carolina but lived in Missouri from 1820 through 1850. Their first-born child and my great uncle, Captain Wesley Riden, had been born in South Carolina in 1818. Their second child and my great aunt, Mary Ann Riden, had been born in Saint Genevieve, Missouri. In all, Grandmother Elizabeth had four sons and two daughters with Joe.

The fact that most of the future Riden line would be buried at Rolla (45%) showed that the earliest families moved from a location on the Mississippi River westward into central and southwest Missouri. Before moving to Rolla, the Riden family claimed residence in Birch Tree, Missouri, site of the Old Baptist Cemetery which I found in shambles. Grave stones could not be recognized. The entire site looked to be covered in foliage. I remembered feeling brain-dead by the reality that my ancestors in the Old Baptist graveyard had vanished. Undeniably, they had returned to an Earth that once gave them life.

Son of Joseph Warren Riden Jr. and Julia Ogle, Private Horace Allen Riden was my great grandfather. Buried at Rolla, the Great Spirit blessed Horace and his wife Alice Sophronia Johnston with six children, one of which became my first-generation grandfather, Charles Ralph Riden. Alice came from the notable Hawkins family tree. After serving in World War I, Horace died accidently while working in the train yards of St. Louis. Research on Horace revealed that Charles' wife Hazel carried the invented maiden name of Johnston. Hazel's true name at birth appeared to be Bronaugh which connected to the Bailey's who claimed Cherokee-Choctaw ancestry.

The official burial site of Captain Wesley Riden turned out to be a matter of scrutiny which fed conspiratorial theory. Newer Riden generations appeared to be perplexed as to where Wesley's body had been finally laid to rest. He was rumored to have died near Old Hopewell on McCortney Hollow Road and buried at the Burnett Cemetery. Some family members believed that Wesley had been buried in the Warren-McCortney Cemetery in Pulaski County not far from where he was killed. Where the captain had been killed and where he had been buried absolutely conflicted. Captain Riden would eventually become a black butterfly (See poem).

The road and the cemetery were 21 miles apart. Wesley had been cut in half by cannon. I could therefore not accept the notion that a rider carried body parts that far away. My personal analysis became such that the Burnett Cemetery held an empty grave. For that matter, who was going to pick up guts, arms and fingers and take them to Warren-McCortney? Almost immediately, I began to question the whereabouts of the graves of my newborn cousins?

Needless to say, I encountered contradictory reports about the location of Wesley's burial location in connection with his death site. The manner of his death and those of the two infant children, James and Sarah, offered signs that their physical remains might be located in the Warren-McCortney Cemetery, which now lay in a field near the banks of the Big Piney River. An analysis of 33 burials at the Warren-McCortney Cemetery however revealed only a single child listed, Mattie Elizabeth Riden, who had died at the age of four. I found her middle name quite interesting and wondered if nominally this had been a tribute or reference to Elizabeth Garrett Riden?

Cumulatively, I found nine Burnett cemeteries in Missouri that could have or did hold Riden family members. Although the Burnett Cemetery in Licking, Missouri was said to contain Wesley's remains as well as the bodies of my fourth-generation grandparents, Joseph and Elizabeth Riden Sr., if Wesley's children, who were believed to have been killed with him had also been buried with him, they were not discoverable at Burnett-Licking. In fact, only one infant burial site existed which was listed as unknown. Summarily, the graves of James and Sarah appeared to be completely missing. They literally became ghosts that I would never find.

Clues surfaced in a project conducted by Waynesville School spanning the years 1997 to 2004. At the time, I had not met with Professor Terry Primas who conducted the project. Later, he would become someone I would encounter by accident. Using a longitudinal approach, the Primas team of researchers discovered over 45 fieldstone markers in the Warren-McCortney Cemetery. The graveyard lay close in proximity to the Big Piney River.

During the evolution of the 1800s cemeteries in the West, grave arrangements varied across subcultures. Some families buried ancestors with stones, an Irish and Native American tradition. Because Wesley and the children did not have a headstone at the Burnett Cemetery, it seemed minimally possible that the Warren-McCortney Cemetery maintained their bodies marked by fieldstones. My grave counting had turned mysteriously intense.

Informal conversations I had with relevant others delineated toward the Riden deaths being only a myth. I did not buy-in to that thought. The Riden deaths appeared shadowy, as though people had been keeping secrets. I supposed that people took confidences with them in death.

Generally speaking, most families accumulated conundrums over the course of successive generations, told through oral tradition. Star witness for the prosecution, Jessie Fern Hatley Riden recalled the night she was lying in bed and heard the familiar sound of an idling motor up the road near the Oak Grove country schoolhouse across from the cemetery. For a brief moment, she hesitated and did not think much of it until flames danced their way through the backdrop of her bedroom window. Fire in the bell tower signaled that the school had become engulfed.

My mother, then a child, was too scared to tell anyone about the motor she heard running in those early morning hours. Yet indeed, she held the poison pen to nail the trespasser slash arsonist. She further explained that the city folk of Stilwell, Oklahoma wanted all children in the area to attend school in town. Her story noted a transitional period in education leading to the death of one-room country schools and the growth of public schools.

The burning of the schoolhouse was an inside job, an example of small-town politics. To this day, Hatley Riden has refused to divulge whose car motor she heard, a furtive that she has maintained for over 70 years. She will take the secret to her grave. I included this story because all families shared unique surprises in their family trees.

It was no secret that I had a great grandmother named Mary Francis Booth (1836-1915) on the Collins' side of genetics. President Abraham Lincoln had been assassinated by John Wilkes Booth. I became rather concerned of a family tie, to say the least. And then the Garrett name showed up again while I was counting more graves. It took my work into a different dimension.

In the days following the vicious murder, while on the take, Booth found relief on a farm owned by Richard Henry Garrett of Locust Hill, Virginia. I researched the connection between my paternal great grandfather's lines of descent with Richard. With the exception of one child, all of Leonard M. Garrett's progeny had been born in Pittsylvania, Virginia which was quite a distance away in miles from Locust Hill. Geographical angles revealed that at best, the men could have been cousins. According to the dates of birth, Leonard M. Garrett would have been closer in age to Richard Garrett's father William Garrett from Essex County, Virginia.

On the other side of the family, for several years it had been rumored that the Hatley's of Stilwell shared a genetic tie with Booth. Rumor had it that the Hatley's started out as Vikings (See Erste

Missionen), a far cry from their reputation as neighborly Christians. Apparently, Mary Booth married Civil War ghost, Private Leroy Hatley (1844-1914) who rode with the Ninth Kansas Cavalry. Her parents showed to be Samuel Booth and Elizabeth Johnson (Letter of Mr. James Hatley, January 24, 2007).

Grandma Booth looked to be originally from Virginia. John Wilkes Booth had been born in Maryland. At this point in my work, Grandma Booth's family connection with Lincoln's assassin would remain unsolved. According to the data on Mary's father and my great grandfather, in the United States alone, there were over 340 Sam Booth burials. Moreover, after going back about six generations of great grandparents, I found it easy to get lost. Records started to fade as time periods became earlier and earlier.

An individual became part of a family of many genetic expressions and displayed in subsequent generations. Offspring had four grandparents. Those grandparents each had four grandparents. Things could get large really quick! Genes competed biologically for being the dominant trait expressed depending on one's DNA code. The simpler point here was that one person carried a preferred gene assembly, behaviors, tendencies, and the talents of many ancestors. Interestingly, it did not take long to reach one-hundred ancestors in a person's genetic heritage. At the end of the effort, I felt satisfied that I was able to minimally go five generations into the past. Grave counting helped me do so.

Motivated by Mr. Jess Adair's hush about Cherokee slave graves in the little Oak Grove Cemetery, I pondered over the magnitude of how many burial sites of slaves existed in Eastern Oklahoma and in the Indian Nations. It had been clearly established by writers that slaves came with the families on the Trail. Thus, cultural integration would have naturally occurred. Sturm confirmed the existence of "biological exchange" between African slaves and their

Cherokee masters (2002, p. 69) but that the Nation "passed a series of anti-miscegenation laws to discourage intermarriage" (2002, p. 54). It happened anyway of course.

Any disposition of the slave graves buried in the Oak Grove Cemetery continued to live on officially undiscovered. I would point out that a large blocked mausoleum-like structure stood in the middle of the Oak Grove Cemetery large enough to hold minimally ten bodies. I could not be sure if Mr. Adair had implied that slaves had been buried in the mausoleum or in the ground. I would never know actually. My good friend died at the age of 90 in 2014.

Oak Grove Cemetery and Piney Cemetery in the Goingsnake District could be claimed as Native American cemeteries dominated by full and mixed blood Cherokee families loyal to the Confederacy. An individualized look at each family and each grave could corroborate such an assessment. Ironically, Oak Grove would one day become my own burial site. I was honored that thus far, five of my close relatives had been interred with the Cherokee in Oak Grove.

Judge John Thompson Adair's (1871-1953) family had been buried at Oak Grove but the magistrate had been interred in Tahlequah. Interestingly, the Starr family showed up in the Adair genes by way of the graves at Oak Grove. I was surprised to find the judge's wife Penelope Starr Mayfield Adair buried at Oak Grove away from her husband. I briefly tracked the famous western hero Belle Starr in order to establish a family connection between the Starr and Adair families as well as the Starr and Hatley families but nothing was uncovered. Nevertheless, Oak Grove Cemetery proved to be an Oklahoma cemetery with profound historical value.

I returned to the Primas Project that had restored the Warren-McCortney graveyard because it offered some family indications as well as clarifications. The background on the project spoke of a gentleman named W.W. McDonald who had served with Captain

John Dent's Company under the supreme command of General Sterling Price in the Mexican-American War. I found W.W. to mean William Walton McDonald born in 1821 and buried at Big Piney Cemetery in Pulaski County. His history appeared quite interesting. Additionally, his photograph could be found online.

In the war against Santa Ana, Private W.W. McDonald had served as a farrier in Bravo Company, Second Mounted Rifles, also known as Second Mounted Volunteers, also known as DeKalb Rangers (Missouri Digital Heritage, Soldiers' Records, 2017a). McDonald's Record of Service Card showed that he joined Bravo Company on May 30, 1846 committing to a twelve-month tour, mustered into service on June 12 at St. Louis, and ultimately served under General Price until June 30, 1847 (MDH, SR, 2017).

Among his many accomplishments, according to Primas, McDonald built the Missouri Old Stage Coach Stop in Waynesville. The project record showed that McDonald had two wives in his life but did not share the same burial locations with either.

At one time, McDonald farmed McCortney-Hollow which happened to be where Captain Wesley Riden fell. Secondly, he became a postmaster like my great grandfather Joseph Sr. Both became political leaders and held occupations in the law circuit. Thirdly, Archibald McDonald had a mill on the Big Piney River close to where the Riden's lived. The McDonald's may have known about the Riden killings in 1864. During the Civil War, McDonald worked as a circuit clerk and county clerk. He had turned 40-years old when the Civil War started.

Age wise, W.W. McDonald looked to be one year older than my great grandfather Captain William Charles Riden, who according to US Census data lived with his father and mother, Joseph Warren Riden Sr. and wife Elizabeth at the Township 34 Range 10 farm in Pulaski County near the Big Piney River. Census data further revealed that by 1860, William Riden had solely inherited the Riden property in the community that would eventually be known as Duke, Missouri.

I suspected that McDonald and my great grandfather knew each other. I could say the same thing for Captain Wesley Riden who would have been roughly 2.5 years older than McDonald. Because the men looked to be farming neighbors, I wondered if McDonald knew about the tension growing between Captain Riden and his father. Something private had happened within the Riden family because younger brother William's good fortune which included taking possession of the farm and Riden's Cave put his older brother Wesley on the outs. Considering a deeper construct, I speculated if the inheritance situation had been tied to Wesley's rebellious opinions and activities? I even contemplated over the idea that Wesley had been involved in Bleeding Kansas and that's why Joseph Sr. did what he did.

I noticed that in 1880 when McDonald relocated to Southeast Pulaski County, William Riden relocated also to Cold Spring in Phelps County. Captain William Riden's son James Wesley Riden, found buried in the Watts Cemetery with many family members (See IMG3), received the property and cave at Big Piney and lived there from 1880 until his death.

Captain William Charles Riden had honored his brother's name Wesley by giving it to his son as a middle name. The military theme I ran with became the notion that William Charles Riden and William Walton McDonald may have served together in the Mexican-American War. Primas had noted that McDonald used a Bounty Land Warrant from serving with the Missouri Mounted Rifles and I pondered if William had used the same type of certificate for his own property. When I checked to see if in fact Riden and McDonald had served together, no ties could be found. As well, the two men had been buried in different cemeteries. I contended that they knew each other socially, but not militarily.

St. Francois County had been an initial mainstay for the Dent's, Garrett's, and Riden's. Given Primas' clue that John C. Dent was the brother of Julia Dent Grant, wife of General U.S. Grant, I had to explore Nancy Garrett's union with the Dent's. I would not have been at all surprised to find that Julia's loyalty with the Union through her husband in a family that sided with the Confederacy may have caused issues between the families. Nancy Garrett Dent (1790-1863) turned out to be genetically my fourth-generation great aunt.

Born after the Revolution, Nancy Garrett Dent had four children with Mark Dent, the oldest being named Elizabeth either to honor her sister and my great grandmother or Mark's first wife. Mark's first baby, Lewis Dent, originated from his marriage to Elizabeth Ferguson who died in 1818. Mark's second marriage in 1819 to Aunt Nancy 13 years his younger, prospered. Nancy lived 73 years passing away in the Civil War's third year. In 1837 when Mark died, the family had established a large farm in St. Francois County.

I looked for the military records of Mark W. Dent and found that Ancestry.com had locked me out of the information. From what I could find on my own, the following details applied to Dent's commander, the Honorable Alexander McNair, Missouri's first governor: after reading briefly through various Google books, it became my understanding that at the rank of colonel, Alexander McNair led Illinois and Missouri militia mounted forces in the War of 1812.

According to Mark Dent's family profile manager K. M. Hoy, service records substantiated this belief. When Dent took time away from his farm to serve in the War of 1812, he had done so at the mature age of 35 years old. Although I could not correctly pinpoint a rank for Mark Dent, I suspected that he had enrolled in the militia as an officer.

Leonard and Margaret Garrett brought Wesley Garrett (1785-1861) into existence in the years following the great revolt of King

George III. Their son and my oldest great uncle endured an incredible 76 years. Wesley Garrett became a legend in Northwest Arkansas. He died at the beginning of the Civil War so he had been spared the visuals of a country gone wild. Some of the most intense battles of the war took place in his old backyard. Wesley's burial site looked to be Clarksville, Arkansas at the Shady Grove Cemetery. Like his military-oriented father, Wesley Garrett started out in 1815 as a militiaman in Tennessee but soon gained the status as an astute businessman and politician in Johnson County Arkansas.

One of the family generated research journals on Wesley revealed an extensive biography that arguably told the story of Arkansas' greatest governmental leader. Wesley Garrett had succeeded in bringing his wife, Elizabeth Cobb and four sons, the oldest being age 12 and the youngest at age 6, to Missouri before 1820. The first true pioneer of Shady Grove and Clarksville, Arkansas, I was just glad to find he showed up in my family tree. Given the fact that I had failed to find perspicacious military data on both Mark W. Dent and Wesley Garrett, one could have concluded that they had become unfindable ghosts of war. "Cattle die and kinsmen die and so dies one's self [but] one thing I know that never dies [is] the fame of a man's deeds" (Haywood, 1995, p. 94). I likened to think of Dent and Garrett in that way.

Sadly, my alcoholic father Joe Max Riden never knew he had originated from the first pioneering family of Arkansas and Missouri. In fact, he never understood that his own genes shared companionship with the likes of Benjamin Hawkins who himself had served with General Washington and Daniel Boone who had conquered the crossing of the Cumberland Gap. Not once had Max Riden entertained the reality that his first birth name came from a derivative of "Joseph" which to my knowledge started with the hero of Breed's Hill, Dr. Joseph Warren. My dad failed to realize that his ancestors found their place among the ghosts of war.

Every once in a while, you catch a fish that has to be thrown back. That was my father!

CHAPTER THREE

Ghosts of War

Son of Hazel, "Mad Max" Riden had served in the U.S. Navy during WWII. Not wanting to be a swabbie, I signed up to be a jarhead instead (See IMG5&6). After looking at data from war reports covering the thirteen major conflicts America has fought, the Civil War remained the bloodiest and most deadly.

More than 618,000 soldiers died in the American Civil War (Divine et al., 2007, p. 402). That's lots of ghosts running around! Disguised as male soldiers, a significant number of female combatants fought and perished (Shulte, 2013; Blanton & Cook, 2003). In my family, like so many others, war rosters showed that fathers, mothers, sisters, brothers and cousins clashed with each other.

Military service had been regarded as an essential part of patriotism. Garrett's, Riden's, Hatley's and Collins' obliged themselves as infantryman, cavalry riders, militiamen, state guards and possibly special-force raiders with a few company level captains. Most who served in the American Revolution and Civil War came from the enlisted ranks. In Missouri, the Riden's supported General Price and saw the incursion of federal troops as a conquest of their own beliefs in Americanism. Like all wars, good generals proved hard to come by (See The Bearded Men). Uncle Fil would have seen it that way, I think.

Uncle Fil Hancock

Several years after World War I, the U.S. Government sponsored the Works Projects Administration (WPA) which produced writers to record important historical events of the past as well as document the lives of people who lived in the 1800s. Part of the effort included hiring cemetery surveyors like "Buster" Bigby who happened to be a personal friend of Grandmother Hatley. The Missouri Slave Narratives were first recorded and translated between 1936 and 1938. Much of the archived information from Missouri ethnographies had been made into electronic files behind the work of Project Guttenberg in 2011.

Federal writers found the interesting Filmore Taylor Hancock (1851-1944) living at home in Rolla, Missouri. Hancock's and Riden's became neighbors at some point. During the Civil War, Mr. Hancock claimed specificity about the fact that "he wasn't Union and his family did not ever go to Rolla, a Union Headquarters" (WPA 2011, 1937). Mr. Hancock's grave could be found in the Rolla Cemetery among seventeen of my own ancestors. I discovered this only after I had read the Hancock narrative.

Folks referred to Mr. Hancock as "Uncle" Fil. A barber by profession, I found him to be quite the child war historian. His narrative denoted that at birth he had been named after two U.S. President's, Millard Fillmore and Zachary Taylor (WPA, 2011, 1937). When he was ten years old, Uncle Fil witnessed the Civil War arrive in Missouri. Uncle Fil had been one of only a few people who could describe an observation of a "living" General Nathaniel Lyon before the Battle of Wilson's Creek and one of a "dead" general after the fighting had ceased. The general's body, once removed from the battlefield, was being sent home Hancock recalled:

In 1861, I saw General Lyon when he passed right by our house… Union soldiers had to pass by our house [during] the time of war. We lived on the main wagon road from Rolla to Springfield… [After he died] they kept him in an icehouse in a spring owned by a man named Phelps. He lived west of Springfield. They kept General Lyon two weeks before they brought him down this way. They shipped him out of Rolla to Connecticut… (WPA, 2011, 1937).

Lyon became the first general to get killed in the Civil War. The area Uncle Fil had described became Phelps County. Uncle Fil had been too young to sign up during the war.

Nothing in Uncle Fil's words, transcribed by the federal writers, pointed to him actually taking up arms and fighting. In his background, Uncle Fil had a slave master by the name of Old Colonel Hancock, which included the Collins family tree. I did not find a connection to the colonel in my lineage of Collins'. Uncle Fil's history died with him when he passed away during World War II. His description of General Lyon made Uncle Fil a hero.

By the time civil conflict stretched its snarly paws into Missouri, the state had already been reeling from political and social upheaval caused by John Brown and Bleeding Kansas. Missouri was combusting and in the throes of chaos. Rampant lawlessness and bushwhacking became regular paying jobs for outlaws. It was also a period when the Ku Klux Klan rode the streets and back roads, especially at night, tormenting families. To complicate matters further, Confederate and Union forces had been harassing plantation owners and slaves, mainly for something to eat, horses, chicken eggs, hogs, turkeys, hay, and money (WPA Reports, 2011, 1936).

The armies weren't simply asking for supplies. Yankees and Rebels were taking what they wanted at will. Naturally, many people became terrified. Missouri's slave populations dealt with the Ku Klux

Klan and civil unrest in the same way all Missourians had thus far: They had to adapt to an environment gone mad.

With passion and objectivity, I spent several days analyzing and categorizing the statements made by the former Missouri slaves in Part I of the 1936 WPA file. It became important for me to discern whether or not my ancestors had practiced slavery. Fourteen pages of detailed notes were then taken.

At the end of the reading, in my mind, I felt that I had gained a concise perspective on what the WPA interviewers were looking for through the answers the respondents had provided. These areas dealt with the following: demographic information, master-slave relationship, punishment, Civil War observations of troop movement and behavior, freedom after Emancipation, employment opportunity, religion, spirituality and haunts and voting behavior. I also found material covering supernatural beliefs in hoodoo.

Of the eighty-two ethnographies conducted by the WPA, seven military veterans provided testimony about their service period during the Civil War (WPA Report, 2011, 1936). Analytically, the following conclusions had been reached: in the data, there were more individual female respondents than male respondents. When President Lincoln announced the Emancipation Proclamation, male slaves left their farms to join up with the Union and Confederacy, the majority of which signed on with the former. Many went up the Mississippi River to Illinois and Ohio to enlist.

Often frightened to death, war affected female slaves and their children. Slaves hid in the woods when soldiers and bushwhackers approached. Some were known to help hide their masters because bushwhackers frequented plantations looking for money and horses. The majority of the slaves favored the Confederate troops over the Union troops passing through. This seemed to be the collective agreement in the narratives. Yet, masters made the slaves cook for both armies.

Sometimes, masters were forced to heed their smokehouse and pantry. To secure the safety of the plantation, masters were known to admit loyalty to both sides, especially when opposed forces were camped nearby. Both the Confederacy and the Union pilfered food, poultry, and cattle from many farms. Each side took horses from the masters with no compensation. Their inclination had been to reconnoiter chests of gold and silver which they believed the masters had hidden. The Civil War nurtured a rebirth in barbarianism.

In the stories, kids were often used as lookouts for soldiers trudging up a road and for reporting unusual activity in the woods. In 50% of the narrative content, respondents discussed seeing famous soldiers passing through their plantations such as General Price, Colonel Marmaduke, and General Lyon as mentioned earlier. Approximately 30% of the respondents remembered hearing the sounds of gunfire and artillery close to their plantations. It was how people learned to seek out safe haven. The Revolution that my great grandfather and uncle served in proved to be a much different war.

Privates Leonard M. Garrett and John W. Garrett

It was not mere coincidence that the Garrett and Riden families shared an original heritage of accomplishment in the new country of America. They worked hard to be successful citizens and agriculturalists during colonial life, had fought and bled with General George Washington against the British, and had without hesitation unselfishly provided for the proclivity of the early Republic.

Verifiable on Valley Forge Muster Rolls, two Garrett ancestors, a great grandfather by the name of Private Leonard M. Garrett and great uncle by the name of Private John W. Garrett (1758-1814) had served with the Continental Army and survived the difficult conditions at Valley Forge, Pennsylvania as well as Morristown, New Jersey. If my genes had failed to survive the winter encampments of Washington's Army during the Revolutionary War, I would not be a human being on Planet Earth. America might not have been a country, if not for my ancestors.

According to Stewart (2008), some of the soldiers at Valley Forge found the need "to boil and eat their shoes" because they were so hungry (p. 86). Confirmed by military records from Archives of Maryland Online, the Garrett brothers conquered the impossible by taunting death and surviving the Revolution. The men never left their posts nor did they ever desert like so many others.

In late 1776 when companies began forming in Maryland, volunteers from several counties including Queen Annes Parish Prince George's County where my ancestors resided signed on to serve three-year enlistments. The Garrett's attached to the 1st Maryland Brigade led by Brigadier General Thomas Smallwood.

While statistically most veterans were of English descent, the ranks also included persons of African, American Indian, Austrian, Dutch, French, German, Irish, Polish, Portuguese, Prussian, Scottish, Spanish, and Swedish descent (Valley Forge Muster Roll Project, 2015). The official enlistment period for the Garrett brothers showed to be from February 25, 1777 to February 29, 1780 (Archives of Maryland Online). The dates of service meant that the Garrett's had been trained by Major General Frederich von Steuben, Washington's right-hand expert.

Stewart (2008) noted that von Steuben first appeared at Valley Forge in February 1778 (p. 86). His record of service had been seconded by the Valley Forge Muster Roll Project. From the Muster Rolls and Other Records of Service of Maryland Troops in the

American Revolution Volume 18, a page viewable in the file Records of Maryland Troops in the Continental Service revealed that Leonard and John had successfully completed their tours of duty and mustered out of the 1st Brigade as time expired (p. 114).

Limited but informative data showed that Private Leonard Garrett had arrived in camp when he was 19 years old and was listed on the January 1778 roll call (VFMRP, 2015). Private John Garrett could also be found "on guard" and listed (VFMRP, 2015). Spring 1778 was a recruiting and signing period for the Continentals. It was a time when General's Washington and von Steuben reoriented and reequipped the Army. These were tough times indeed, considering the fact that in the spring of 1778, bacterial disease had crippled Washington's Army more so than the frigid conditions (VFMRP, 2015).

The Fighting Third had been part of a combat-tested brigade-level force which had participated in the battles of New York, New Jersey, Brandywine, Germantown, Monmouth, and in the capture of Savannah, Georgia. According to reliable information, the Garretts' company commander listed out to be 1st Lieutenant Horatio Claggett.

By 1779, the Revolutionary War became a stalemate of wills. The winter quarters at Morristown turned out to be much harsher than that of Valley Forge but the company endured. Honorably discharged, I parlayed electronically with a Valley Forge Park Ranger who informed me that the Maryland troops had been memorialized on site (Mr. M. Di Paolo, Personal Communications, June 27, 2017).

General Washington had been quoted as saying, "Happiness and moral duty are inseparably connected" (Chesapeake Illustrated, 2010, p. 10). Remembering my own experience with commissioned officers, I envisioned the general discussing such matters with my ancestors. Following his service period, records indicated that Private Leonard M. Garrett bought sizable property in Greenville County

South Carolina in 1805. According to Henderson and Ancestry.com Roots Web (2004), Private Garrett purchased 200 acres of land on December 27. His brother John W. Garrett returned to Virginia after the war where he owned 25 acres of land in Pittsylvania County.

Born in Pennsylvania, Daniel Boone (1734-1820) became a character in Missouri's rich history. Sources writing on Boone remarked that his advance across the Cumberland Gap had been met by bands of young Indian warriors where members of the party had been killed including his oldest son, James (Bryan & Rose, 1876). Records on the pioneer families of Missouri provided by Bryan and Rose (1876) hinted at the possibility that my ancestors knew Daniel Boone's children (p. 6). All three families arrived in Missouri around the same time frame. Leonard Garrett became my family's Daniel Boone. Grandfather Riden Sr. became a justice in Boone County.

Private Leonard Garrett and his extended family survived the long trek to Missouri through unknown lands dominated by Native Americans. At Valley Forge, the Garrett's had served under a commander of Cherokee heritage. As well, the Pendleton District of South Carolina where Garrett's and Riden's lived from 1805 to 1819 had originally been a Cherokee area. Although strongly inferred, General Smallwood may have had influence in Leonard Garrett's decision to move to South Carolina in the first place. When he relocated to Missouri, Leonard Garrett had established camaraderie with the Cherokee. The trip to Missouri would have taken the Garrett's and Riden's through Cherokee Territory which provided a measure of safety I would think.

The Missouri pioneer movement actually predated the famous Donner Party Expedition. What motivated the Garrett's and Riden's to emigrate across terrain that in the 1800s would have offered a tremendous physical challenge for a crew and wagon? Religion may have been one of the reasons that inspired the families to take on pioneering. Family graves provided important clues.

Grandfather Joseph Warren Riden Jr., son of Captain William Charles Riden, died of abdominal tuberculosis in 1912. His grave could not be recovered although the gravesite itself, the Old Baptist Cemetery, had been found at Birch Tree, Missouri. The site looked to be grossly covered in thick impenetrable brush, vines, and trees. The "Old Baptists" turned out to be one of the first pioneer religious groups to flourish in Missouri. Some flocks referred to them as "Ironsides" or "Hardshell Baptists" (Bryan & Rose, 1876, p. 81). I remembered being appalled at the graveyard conditions.

Certainly, the Ozarks offered unimaginable beauty, forestry, farming and mining. I conceded to the thought that the opening of the West tickled Leonard Garrett to relocate but I also began to comfort myself on the following points: if Leonard owned 200 acres of land in South Carolina from 1805 to 1817 but did not involve himself in plantation slavery, as the record showed, then he may have ventured to Missouri to get away from it all together. Several records were clear to me that the Garrett's and Riden's had a lot of land but they did not own a plantation.

Ultimately, my ancestors became motivated by a spirit of frontiersman sweeping the country called Manifest Destiny. Intuition told me that my great grandfather went to Missouri to become a timberman. By 1820, around the time of the Missouri Compromise and seventeen years after the Louisiana Purchase, the Garrett's and Riden's began showing up in Missouri records and documents. As the forests grew in Southeast Missouri, so did the mills.

Great Grandfather Leonard Garrett died in 1826 leaving his legacy to me through his daughter and my great grandmother, Elizabeth Garrett Riden, wife of Justice Joseph Warren Riden Sr. of Texas County, Missouri. Leonard's oldest son and my great uncle,

Wesley Garrett, became a successful coroner, legislator, and U.S. Postmaster in Arkansas Territory. Captain Wesley Riden had received his name at birth to recognize and honor his famous uncle Wesley Garrett who in 1833 while serving in the Arkansas territorial legislature had drafted the bill establishing Johnson County.

Husband of Elizabeth Cobb, Wesley Garrett died in the same year the Civil War began, and found buried at the Shady Grove Cemetery in Clarksville, Arkansas (Hoy, 2017, No. 2445). Leonard's gravesite was believed to be located in the Hamilton Cemetery in Bismarck, Missouri. I was not able to secure John's burial site at present.

The Garrett's first came to America in the middle 1600s and showed to be one of the first families of Virginia to own a business. Grandmother Elizabeth had been born in colonial Virginia in a place called Pittsylvania. Many of the early families who came westward were families of war veterans taking advantage of their post-war benefits.

Military service became a legacy in the Garrett-Riden and Collins-Hatley families. Many served in combat. Many bit the bullet. Those that survived war found success after their enlistments. A select few went on to become sheriffs. I scanned the genetic relationship between myself and famous lawman Patrick Floyd Garrett (1850-1908). The Garrett family roots that arrived in Virginia did so by way of England.

The Commonwealth of Virginia was the prototype of a new America. The Garrett lineage had originated from Lord John Garrett I in England (Garrett, 2009). During the research, I was able to locate a John Garrett (1794-1852) listed by Find a Grave.com 2015a as Pat Garrett's great grandfather who was born in North Carolina and died in Alabama. According to Garrett (2009), John was listed as a land lottery winner in 1827 and became a successful farmer in Georgia and then in Chambers County, Alabama (p. 8).

The Garrett's in my family heritage had never lived in Alabama or Georgia to my knowledge. If I had any family relationship with Pat Garrett, it would have begun with John Garrett II (1631-1706) who had immigrated to Virginia from England (Garrett, 2009). It became at least possible that Pat and I shared a similar blood line of English tradition. A believable common ancestor heritage with Pat Garrett showed up in the records arranged by Garrett (2009, p. 1-8). The first and second names of William, Henry, Thomas, and Elizabeth appeared to be popular in my family lineage and this was observed to be similar in John II's family also. Indeed, the evidence seemed to associate with specificity, the names William, Thomas, and Elizabeth. However, real confusion crept in when I attempted to decipher all first named John's.

John Garrett II had married twice and had a total of seven children. Five of the seven children had been born in Virginia, the oldest birthed in 1674 and the youngest in 1680. Only one child, Thomas Garrett, had died outside of Virginia in the State of North Carolina which happened to be where Pat Garrett's great grandfather had been born. It seemed to me that Pat Garrett's blood line had originated from Thomas Garrett. This point was then corroborated by the research of Garrett (2009) which explained partly that Pat's family members had migrated to North Carolina, Alabama, Louisiana, and Georgia.

Because my grandmother Elizabeth Garrett Riden had been born in Virginia, it was possible that her ancestors originated from one of the four Garrett families that had been born in, had lived in, and had stayed in and later died in Virginia. Grave records of an English birth heritage and death record in America looked to be spotty however. Many of the earliest graves of immigrants were marked unknown, thus creating dead-ends.

Charles Riden immigrated from England to Maryland in the year 1664 (Filby & Meyer, 1985). The name-heritage of Riden was Anglo-Saxon. The first name of Charles had been passed along through the generations in honor of King Charles 1645. In 1840, most Riden families could be found living in Missouri, however, by 1920 the majority of relatives resided in Pennsylvania and the South. The initial impression I had of this finding was one of antithetical value. The Riden's moved westward in 1819 as a pioneer family and dispersed across the North American landscape but after the Civil War had been discovered to be more concentrated on the East Coast. Riden genes had taken up residence in thirty-eight states with notable concentrations in Ohio, Illinois, Texas, Iowa, Tennessee, and Georgia but after the Civil War and the Industrial Revolution, more families resided in New York and Pennsylvania.

Through the Pioneer Spirit, in the beginning years of 1800, emigrants of Garrett's and Riden's directly helped establish and prosper the states of Arkansas and Missouri. Historically, the Garrett-Riden generations became hardworking community-driven citizens. The family trees that blossomed from the union between my great grandparents, Elizabeth and Joseph Riden, presented a unique aspect of history that had been previously overlooked.

Representative of a new America, the Riden's and their descendant families became teachers, preachers, farmers, and soldiers. They worked in the railroad yards and on the Mighty Mississippi. Riden genes evolved and mixed with nearly one-hundred different families including Ashworth, Bailey, Bean, Blankenship, Bryant, Buckner, Grace, Hargiss, Huff, Hood, Keeney, McCortney, Nickless, Ogle, Payne, Roden, Steppat, Thornton, Welch, Whitaker, Wilson, and Woods. Bean was a Cherokee name. Payne was a surname connected to David Payne who helped establish the area located in Stillwater at Oklahoma State University. Hood was a prominent surname in the Riden family tree whose descendants moved into Oklahoma and as far west as California in the early 1900s. In some families like the Buckner's and Keeney's, family-to-family brother and sister tandem marriages showed to be common. Many of these families endured the hardships of rampant disease, infant and childhood mortality, civil war, world war, a dust-bowl and the Great Depression.

Although I had a great grandmother named Elizabeth and a great grandfather named William Charles, I had never known my family of Riden's to be of high royalty or owners of castles. The Hatley's did but that was the other side of the family. Oppositely, I had never heard of the Riden's living in caves even though we owned one. Guided by the 1922 Smithsonian Institute Report, Fowke (2006) recognized the discovery of Riden's Cave:

> A mile southeast of the steel bridge across Big Piney on the Edenville Road is Riden's Cave, in a small ravine opening into another ravine. The entrance is 25 feet wide and 8 feet high, and the front chamber extends 30 feet to an abrupt turn. There are large rocks on the floor near the mouth and some cave earth and a small amount of refuse at the front. It was never occupied except as a temporary camp (p. 57).

According to Fowke (2006, p. 16), the Riden cave was probably used during intermittent times out of a need for shelter based on the structural features of refuse and cave earth. Refuse signaled the material ordinarily found on the site of an Indian Village (Fowke, p. 16). Cave earth was found in the front chambers of large caverns where minute amounts of clay and soil had been carried inside by animals (Fowke, p. 16). Strategically, I was sure that my Confederate ancestors of Riden heritage found the Ozark Uplift caves necessary for protection against bushwhackers and invaders like the Union Army. To this day, however, I had been unable to prove the Riden's actually used the cave system for safety.

Born at Birch Tree, Missouri in Hutten Valley, Ashland oilman Charles Ralph Riden (1903-1974) became my first-generation grandfather who was living in Oklahoma City when he died. Like my father, I really never knew him. I watched him pick weeds out of his yard once but we never embraced. His wife and my grandmother, Hazel J. Riden, also known as Hazel J. Johnston and Hazel J. Bronaugh lived a very self-centered, secluded life. I remembered meeting her one time at the age of ten in a café. Cumulatively, I recalled spending about two hours of my life with Charles and Hazel. In 2015, I was not at all surprised or even angered to find myself completely disinherited. My grandfather had been too young to serve in WWI and too old to serve in WWII.

Upon her husband's passing, Hazel got everything. In the documents that I viewed at the Oklahoma City Court Clerk's Office, Charles Riden had specified that he was leaving my father and uncle "absolutely nothing." Hazel received the home they lived in, 1000 shares of Ashland Oil Company stock, and $25,000 in cash. If I were to describe my dad's mother in one word, that term would be 'greedy.'

Admittedly, Hazel Riden appeared to be deceptively cunning. For most of her life, she told people she met that she came from Georgia and had been related to the famous Civil War General Joseph Eggleston Johnston. That turned out to be a lie. Hazel actually picked up the maiden name Johnston for an unknown reason from my grandmother Alice Sophronia Johnston who married Horace Allen Riden. Alice and Hazel were not related.

I looked for the Bronaugh connection and found the family name tied to the Bailey's in Northeast Oklahoma. The Bailey family had been listed in numerous spots on the Dawes Rolls. I discovered a Cherokee woman by the name of Hazel J. Bailey, Card No. 3640, Roll No. 8858. Per the facts, Hazel Riden's middle name had been "Jennie." A white man by the name of James Franklin Bronaugh married Jennie G. Bailey, the latter having quite a few siblings. All had been buried in the Oakwood Cemetery in Mounds, Oklahoma. What made this story interesting was the fact that my father had been buried at Oakwood thus displaced from the graves of his immediate family. I think most of the people in my dad's life hated him.

Adding to the drama, it looked minimally possible that Hazel had a degree of Cherokee blood. However, if Hazel's gene pool evolved from Native American descendants, it had never been discussed by my father to my mother. It became hard to put down the idea that Hazel had hidden her own heritage for reasons I could never truly understand. But to be clear, I grew disgusted by it.

A rehearsed social decision in the early 1900s, Native Americans had been prone to hide their background for fear of discrimination. One truth could be emphasized without hesitation: for some reason Hazel Riden did not want to be known as Bronaugh so she picked a maiden name arbitrarily from her husband's family. My intuitions led me to believe that Hazel shunned-away her Indian inheritance entirely. Because she was selfish and absorbed by materialism, she chose to be a white woman instead. I could not respect her thinking on the matter.

Fortunately, Hazel Riden became a speck of dust in my life. Ashamed of her, I refocused my attentions back on Missouri. During the sleepless hours of my investigations, the more I read the more I began to realize that a lot of Missourians were deeply divided on the slave issue generations before the Missouri Compromise had ever been reached. My initial impression was that the Riden's were not practicing the abomination of slavery.

It had been affirmed that two servants accompanied the Garrett's and Riden's to Missouri. From the census reports, I grew confident that a father and son worked for the two families. I considered motherly separation which happened often during the dark days of slavery. From the narratives I read, I was never able to align Missouri slave plantations and their owners with the families whatsoever. In Missouri Slave Narratives, Volume X, nothing had been discovered socially and geographically.

Using google maps of Pulaski and Phelps County relative to St. Louis and the Mississippi River, and saddled with notes taken from slave narratives and the locations of slave quarters, the Riden's arguably lived in the western area of Missouri's centrally-located plantation system. Where one resided in relation to the Mississippi River was important in comprehending where the Missouri slave owners lived and went about their business. Several counties along the Mississippi River (St. Louis, St. Charles, Warren, Franklin, Jefferson, St. Genevieve, Perry, Bollinger, Cape Girardeau, and Scott County) were mentioned in stories told by former Missouri slaves. In the records, I never located any Riden's listed as slave masters.

Big Piney could be found on a map in south-central Missouri. In Volume X: Missouri Slave Narratives, nothing was ever mentioned or interpreted that would have led one to believe that the Big Piney River citizens themselves had slaves. If the Riden's owned slaves, the connection seemed to be those who were interred nearer to St. Louis and at Cape Girardeau rather than the Riden's who lived a good distance away from the Mississippi River. Big Piney River was 169 miles west of the old French trading post, Cape Girardeau.

A notable percentage of the male certificates of death that I reviewed on the Garrett's and Riden's inferred that the deceased's practiced the occupation of farming. In the nineteenth century, farmers became societal rock stars and bred large families. Siblings, cousins, brothers, sisters, uncles, aunts and local friends all shared chores to support the farm. A growing nation needed to establish the ability to subsist and farmers to feed the communities (See Barr's The Farmer, p. 13-14).

While it appeared a misnomer that brothers battled brothers in the Civil War, a more precise statement may have been that farmers battled farmers, at least in the West. When war arrived, farmers sat down their pitchforks and tools and put on uniforms. Like many family events dating back to English tradition, the Riden generations became divided by war. It was an ugly side of family heritage. William Riden had a flag on his grave. Wesley Riden did not.

As a vehicle of interpretation, military chronicles became extremely important in linking genetic drift and flow in a prospective family. When I came across Riden veteran records, one of the first things I did was compare soldiers' names with the Missouri records of my family tree. This helped establish similar and dissimilar points of common ancestry. As well, looking at theunits the soldiers had served in assisted in differentiating between families who came West or stayed in the East. War certainly divided the nation along military and economic lines, and as I had expected, drew a line in the sand between Riden and Hatley opinions.

When political diplomacy failed between the Northern and Southern states in 1861, state militias were immediately converted into larger units such companies and artillery batteries, battalions, regiments, and brigades. Lines of loyalty developed most expediently. Commissioned officers on each side of the conflict set about the countryside recruiting able bodied Riden's out of the counties of South Carolina, Virginia, and Pennsylvania.

Distant relative Private W.H. Riden, for example, served in the 2nd South Carolina Infantry Regiment "which established itself as one of the elite shock troop units of Robert E. Lee's Army of Northern Virginia" (FamilySearch.org. 2015). Various sources indicated that W.H. Riden's unit was with the Army of Tennessee at Appomattox when the general surrendered in 1865. Opposed and serving under a Union flag, Private John W. Riden completed a nine-month tour of duty with the 131st Regiment of Pennsylvania.

Soldiers named Riden clashed with each other in major engagements like the Seven Days' Battle, Cold Harbor, and numerous other battles including bloody Gettysburg, Fredericksburg, and the Siege of Petersburg. In a second example, archives showed that Privates George W. Riden, Mastin W. Riden, and W.C. Riden serving under Confederate colors engaged Union Private J.W. Riden at Chancellorsville.

In the research, I always had to be on guard for name-doubles. War records from the Revolutionary War through the Civil War were spotty, broad, and non-specific much of the time. Civil War enlistment cards proved especially difficult. Often the officers filling out the cards had untidy penmanship, used initials instead of full names, and left spaces blank. When initials were recorded, it would take days to associate who they belonged to. Grave markers helped alleviate some of the problem but veterans' graves had environmentally deteriorated making it difficult to extrapolate particulars. Document-wise, there seemed to be a lot about historical battles and less about the men who fought in them. One thing proved solid: more than twenty-eight Riden's served closer to the nation's capital during the Civil War.

Soldiers showed up in the Riden files from the U.S. National Park Service and had to be separated. I assigned individual case numbers and separated the Riden's according to rank, first name or initials, regiment assignment showing state service, and company (See Appendix A).

Overall, the population of men which carried the Riden surname had participated in the Eastern Theater of the Civil War. Of these, the majority (64%) had enlisted in the Union compared to the Confederate States (36%). According to rank, there were no commissioned officers noted. In the enlisted ranks, most (79%) had served in the lowest grade, private (E-1). A small percentage (21%) had attained the status of non-commissioned officer. Unit assignments showed to reflect brothers and cousins (7 sets). Type of military job appeared to show that most of the Riden's served as infantrymen (82%) where I anticipated that casualty rates would be high. State affiliation looked to be the most telling qualitative statistic. Unit and recruitment locations turned out to be particularly important. I broke down states accordingly: Pennsylvania had the largest faction of Riden enlistees (50%) followed by Georgia (25%), South Carolina, Missouri, Kentucky, Illinois (14%) and Tennessee (11%).

The Riden's clearly viewed the Civil War differently. One could infer that the mainstream of Riden-named soldiers viewed serving the Union as the best option. Not true for Missouri whose farmers sided with the Confederacy. It appeared agreeable that the Riden's appreciated a hero of the Revolution, Dr. Joseph Warren. A man by the name of Joseph Warren Riden Sr. became my fourth generation great grandfather. General Warren gave his life for his country on the top of a hill in 1775 which for the record had been three years before Leonard and John Garrett enlisted.

Dr. Joseph Warren

One of the stimulating storylines that arose in my work focused on how parents named their children after American icons. Soldiers, politicians and people in power all showed to be traditional choices for first and middle names. Child-naming evolved into social, political and religious avowals. Naming clearly could be construed as a military preference. In the American colonies, we know of course that a person was either a Patriot or Loyalist. Through the process of naming, parents picked which side they were on through their children.

Dr. Joseph Warren was KIA six days after his thirty-fourth birthday. In my own family tree, the name's Charles, Joseph, William, and Warren were propertied. The name Charles fancied traditional French and Germanic values. The designation Joseph signaled the family tie to Christianity. William became a name associated with military service and conquest. Warren looked to be a name the Riden's wanted to display with distinction.

It became my primary belief that my great grandfathers who carried the name Joseph Warren Riden had been named so to honor Major General Dr. Joseph Warren (1741-1775) who was killed during combat on Breed's Hill. Reverence paid to patriots of the Revolution signaled that the Riden family members were themselves compatriots of a new America. I could only imagine that when Grandmother Elizabeth told her father, Leonard Garrett, that she wanted to marry Riden, he would have been jubilant in his demeanor.

The Riden's apparently thought a lot of the physician-general formally of Massachusetts and the hero of Breed's during the American Revolution who fought bravely and helped lead the battling Continentals against wave-upon-wave of British infantry. The Warren name had descended from the royal families of England and France. Unfortunately, I was never able to genetically bond the Warren's with the Riden's in Virginia.

The Warren's buried in the Warren-McCortney Cemetery at Big Piney, Missouri proved to be too young to be connected with the Riden habit of naming their offspring Joseph Warren. From Primas' Report, Warren birthdates looked to be in the 1840s. Census showed that by 1839, the Riden's already held property in Pulaski County. Therefore, the Riden's brought the Warren name with them from South Carolina. It was possible that surnamed Warren's traveled to Missouri with the Riden's in 1819 but that could not be proven.

According to Wildrick (2009), the Warren's had established themselves as one of America's first families displaying patriotic service in farming, soldiering, and politics among a host of other qualities. Dr. Warren had been vastly admired, remembered for his medical work against smallpox and his larger-than-life speeches given annually in Boston at the site of the Boston Massacre (Wildrick, p. 27-28). Dr. Warren played a huge role in political activism ultimately inspiring Revolution (Wildrick, p. 28). His writings about the Stamp Act helped inspire the formation of the Sons of Liberty (Wildrick, p. 28). Warren had been elected President of the Third Provincial Congress, but shortly after being commissioned as a Major General, had been killed on Breed's (Wildrick, p. 28).

The family connection of Riden-Warren needed to be clarified. Giving one's own child the middle name of the surname of another family showed honor and reverence. Indeed, it meant something special. For what, I did not initially comprehend until later in the research. For an investigative mind, tracking down the relationship potentially made for a unique and interesting story. One fact remained absolute and without deterrence: The Riden's praised the Warren's before Missouri.

I had heard of Warrensburg, Missouri so I pondered over the Missouri relationship. Had a family bond been built due to historical events such as the passage of the Kansas-Nebraska Act, Bleeding

Kansas, the John Brown Raid, or other related troubles between the pro-slavers and anti-slavers of the Free Soil Party? The only Warren connection in Missouri that remained relevant was the location of the Warren-McCortney Cemetery close to where my great uncle and cousins fell. Riden's in my family had no burial site in Johnson County where the Warren's

In Missouri alone, of the 3,824 Warren burial sites I looked into, over half had been interred before 1900 when the influx of settlers arrived in Warrensburg. There were 263 listed sites marked before 1800. Therefore, Warrensburg had been one of the earliest models of a frontier city in the West with the majority of population growth in the 1800s.

The distance between South Carolina and Missouri calculated to be 792 walking miles away from each other, capital to capital. The trip would have taken a family through the Chattahoochee Forrest and Chattanooga across terrain owned by the Cherokee of Georgia and Tennessee which would have allowed for a safe journey. Tennessee, Georgia, and South Carolina cemeteries were filled with the burial sites of the Warren's. Indeed, one could have raised an argument that the Warren's were one of the top three oldest families in America.

As a secondary proposition, the name Warren inferred to be associated with state location. Interestingly, when I studied how the Johnston's were gene-linked to the Hawkins family, I soon realized that Warrensburg and the middle name of Warren in the Riden Family Tree had been relevant with Warren County, North Carolina. It appeared that all three sur-names of Riden, Johnston, and Hawkins commonly resided in North Carolina at one time. The linkage in the research spoke volumes for the relevancy of middle names in family trees. Certainly, middle names offered indications to heritage or at least it did in mine.

Upon returning to the Valley Forge Muster Rolls, clues on the Warren-Riden interface surfaced. According to the VFMRP, a total of 11 soldiers with the surname Warren had mustered with the Garrett's at Valley Forge. Nine of these soldiers served in combat units from Massachusetts but two of the men originated from New York and Virginia respectively. According to the official roll, Private Peter Warren of the 12th Virginia Regiment had enlisted one month before Grandmother Elizabeth's father and uncle, Leonard and John Garrett(VFMRP, 2017).

It seemed possible that at least one of the eleven Warren's became acquainted with the Garrett's at Valley Forge because enlistment periods intertwined but also because of the sheer number of soldiers carrying both surnames. Cumulatively, twelve Garrett's had served at Valley Forge (VFMRP, 2017). This did not explain how or why my grandmother Elizabeth Garrett Riden eventually married "Joseph Warren" Riden Sr. in 1817, a full thirty-seven years after her father's service period. The Warren-thing seemed to be specifically a Riden-thing.

The military service thing became a major part of Leonard Garrett's legacy to his family. These gifts would be handed down to his grandson, Captain William Charles Riden and then on to me. The records covering William Charles became arduous to follow but from everything I learned of him, he appeared to be an honorable soldier. I could express with certainty that he possessed excellent horsemanship skills. In war, what good are you if you 'can't ride a horse?' In 2017, I was pleased to learn that Captain Riden had a Cherokee wife.

Captain William Charles Riden

Originally from South Carolina, Joseph Warren Riden Sr. of Lynch Township, Texas County, Missouri fathered Captain William Charles Riden (1822-1906). He was pushed into life by his mother Elizabeth. In 1847, William married Mary Huff (1819-1852) who died at the young age of 32 years old approximately eleven days after giving birth to son James Wesley Riden (1851-1928). Following Mary's death, Captain Riden married Delilah Giddens (1836-1913).

When I visited the captain's grave on June 22, 2016 it had been recently decorated with an American flag. Sources indicated that Captain Riden once served in the Missouri State Guard (MSG). According to Erwin (2013), his commanding general would have been Sterling Price whose MSG unit battled at Wilson's Creek near Springfield, Missouri. Military records showed a W.C. Riden with military service who I believed had to be William Charles.

Digital secondary sources indicated that Captain Riden had been born in two places apparently: St. Francois County, Missouri according to Wikitree or St. Genevieve County, Missouri according to Find a Grave.com 2015b. Conferring to the 1830 U. S. Federal Census provided by Hoy (2017, No. 37), William had lived in St. Francois County. Geographically, both areas lay on the west bank of the Mississippi River. This region along the river reflected its astute French origin. Grandpa William's burial site at Beaver Creek south of Rolla had been confirmed by me and backed up in the U.S. Government War Archives. The location of the grave showed that the Riden's had branched westward into the southern interior of Missouri.

My initial curiosity with this great grandfather pertained to military rank during the Civil War and why he became a captain? The reason for the interrogative centered on leadership and how small Missouri townships responded to federal insurrection. Confederates had to select leaders expediently because the Union Army had taken an offensive posture. It had been perceived that some community leaders were titled (ranked) according to their social stature.

To be selected as captains and sergeants said something about how individuals were regarded in their respective societal groups. Normally, military leaders received officer commissions based on age, education, training, and combat record. Many officers had been the offspring of early pioneers who owned land estates. Both ranked at captain, William and Wesley Riden seemed to fall into this latter category. An original pioneering member that helped establish Boone Township in June 1845, Justice Joseph Riden Sr. laid the groundwork for his sons' military service. When the Civil War began, William and Wesley were in their forties. If anything, the war showed that common men could recruit and build sizable forces.

Erwin's 2013 book explained that initial Union officer commissions were granted based on how many recruits a person "brought into service" (p. 31). This provision changed when Governor Hamilton Gamble reorganized and funded the Union's state militia, giving him the power to "select the colonels, lieutenant colonels and majors" while the troops "elected the captains and lieutenants" (Erwin, p. 33).

At the beginning of the Civil War, Confederate Riden's in Missouri held officer status. By comparison, Union men named Riden from Pennsylvania ranked out with mostly privates. Name searches on "Captain Riden" popped up William Quantrill's name and a list of his 450-man guerilla unit but William Riden's information had not been found on the Quantrill roster. Part of the problem came about in how name searches could be entered. For example, William Charles Riden could be searched as William C. Riden, Will Riden, W. Charles Riden, W.C. Riden, or Wm. C. Riden. In the Quantrill reference, this Riden could have been Wesley.

Geographical analysis helped to locate missing demographic evidence. The U.S. Census Data in 1860 recorded that a "Captain W.C. Riden" could be found residing at Township 34-Range 10, Pulaski County Missouri (Hoy, 2017, No. 37). Moser's Report (undated) showed Captain W.C. Riden would have lived in or near Duke, Missouri with the closest U.S. Post Office at Blooming Rose. The location would be southwest of Rolla. In tracking family movement using mapping and plotting data, I felt confident that this had been the area where Captain Riden once took up homesteading and indeed that became true. Riden's Cave could be found nearby.

Moser discussed the extensive forested region of Pulaski County which helped me develop some thoughts about the Riden family as farmers in that they may have actually worked in the timber industry. Plot maps supplied by Professor Primas showed that Riden's owned extensive properties in Pulaski County and the Big Piney River region, an area dense with arboreal growth. In an unfortunate event, Riden's first wife Mary had a father who was killed by a falling tree in Pulaski County.

What I did not understand was Captain William Riden's role in the 1861 Confederate struggle? From the Goodspeed 1889 County Records of Texas County Missouri, Military Troops and Taxpayer List, three records were found concerning the Riden's from Missouri and military duty during the Civil War. Documents showed that "J.M. Riden" had served in the Confederacy, "W.C. Riden" had served in the MSG, and "Joseph Riden," had been listed as a taxpayer non-soldier. Other historical information showed Joseph in the MSG with his son William. Although rank had not been mentioned, it became my impression that the W.C. Riden rostered herein was Captain William Charles Riden.

My next effort turned into peeling back the pages of Missouri State Guard History to look for more clues about William. As the

Union intruders entered Missouri, community units got shuffled like a deck of cards causing a dreadful lack of accountability. To reiterate one's perspective, by 1861 Missouri was a state in chaos socially and governmentally.

The strategy of using guard forces to support an active standing army occurred during the American Civil War. General Price consolidated various Confederate forces such as the Missouri State Guard which included an understanding with the Cherokee Mounted Rifle Units under General Watie and Colonel Adair. They became the Confederate Army of the West. Governor Gamble had taken the initiative to scramble together a hodgepodge of loose units and volunteers into militias. The Civil War in this sense mirrored the Revolutionary War where citizens served as soldiers and then returned home to carry on their normal duties as farmer and father. Home District Units (HDUs) trained at Cowskin Prairie located in Indian Territory near present day Grove, Oklahoma.

Serving under the command of General Price appeared a pale rider wearing a brigade officer's insignia around his neck. The officer's name happened to be Brigadier General Monroe Mosby Parsons (1822-1865) to be precise, not to be confused with Confederate Gray Ghost, John Singleton Mosby. Trained in law, General Parsons was a combat veteran of the Mexican-American War who went on to serve as the U.S. District Attorney for Western Missouri. When the Civil War broke out in Missouri, Parsons became a leader in the state senate. The war immediately forced him to again take up arms.

General Price dispensed General Parsons to take charge of the MSG Sixth Division and its foray of officers and guardsmen. Captain Riden was thought to have been with Parson's Sixth based on his county of record. The garrisons of the Sixth included Kelly's Infantry, Brown's Cavalry, and Guibor's Field Artillery. Age wise, seven months separated the birthdates of General Parsons and William. If William had served as a captain, he would have been regarded as old by fellow soldiers. One would think that at least based on his birth year of 1822, his war should have been the Mexican-American War. I needed more time to interrogate Sixth Division units as well as combatants who may have fought in 1846.

Captains in the Confederacy commanded at the company level. Republished from 1895, Ohio State University electronic transcripts on the Civil War covering selected serials had been arduously scrutinized in determining which company Riden may have led and what specialty he maintained whether it be artillery, cavalry, or infantry. I found nothing to report with any specificity as to the military service of Riden from this report. Additional searching referenced Goodspeed (1971) where I received nine hits on "Riden" as a surname, one of which had been spelled incorrectly as "Piden." The information appeared family relevant and collaborative:

Page 411   Opening of the Wright County Pioneer School: in 1842, the first school opened at Hartville, Mo. "Jesse" Riden's three to four children were seated among its first pupils.

Page 435   Early Marriage Record of Texas County: on March 1, 1855, Captain William C. Riden married D. Gideon corrected to Cherokee Delilah A. Giddens, his second marriage.

Page 437   Establishment of County Seat, Texas County: in January 1846, commission establishes two forty-acre tracts of land owned by the estates of Joseph Riden and Henry Hawkins.

Page 438   In January 1847, Joseph Riden, his son [John] Wesley Riden, and colleagues petitioned the court to sell school lands. A new courthouse had been authorized to be built.

Page 438   September 1847, Joseph Riden appointed District No. 1 School Clerk.

Page 439   Special Texas County Election, 1856: Joseph Riden replaced James Campbell as Judge.

Page 442   Establishment of Boone Township, 1845: Joseph Riden appointed as Justice.

Page 449   Texas County Congressional Elections, 1856: For Representative, Joseph Riden 267 votes vs. John C. Wood 285 votes.

Page 454   Warfare begins in Texas County, MO in December 1861.

Page 462   Civil War Roster: Joseph Riden was a taxpayer, Captain J.M. (J.W.) Riden was fighting for the Confederacy, and W.C. Riden was listed with MSG.

Page 462   The full name of Captain John Wesley Riden was not listed on a Union or Confederate roster but was recognized with the MSG.

The preceding information aligned with the Goodspeed (1889) information. What the material showed from Missouri Digital Heritage (2007, 1889) about William Charles Riden was not supported by complementary documents. Moreover, the soldiers' database had no listing of a J.M. Riden or Wesley Riden ever serving in the Confederate or Union Army. What I could remark with surety became this reality: the Riden's had a lot to do with building Texas County.

The epicenter of Texas County had been built on former land owned by the Riden and Hawkins families (Goodspeed, p. 437). Both the father Joseph Sr. and his son John Wesley were listed in the county records as land owners (Goodspeed, p. 438-439). Joseph Sr. served as the family politician and had been inducted as a school official, a justice, and a judge (p. 439-449). In 1856, he ran for a state congressional seat but lost by eighteen votes. Military and political leadership appeared to be a common thread on the other side of my family also. While the Riden's had been partial to the Confederacy, the Hatley's in my tree sided with the Union.

Privates Leroy Hatley, Sherrod Hatley, and William Hatley

Cavalry Private Leroy Hatley could be found buried at the Kenney Cemetery in Newton County, Missouri. Born in 1844, he was at the perfect age of 17 when the Civil War began. Sixteen days after enlistment, Leroy's company prepared horses for the Battle of Honey Springs. In September of 1864, he participated in the Second Battle at Cabin Creek against General Watie's Cherokee fighters. Based on the combat record, his service years would be spent fighting to help federal forces gain control of Oklahoma Indian Territory.

Members of Mike Company, Great Grandfather Leroy Hatley and two uncles, Privates Sherrod Hatley and William Hatley, served with distinction in the Union's 9th Kansas Cavalry Regiment based out of Fort Leavenworth, Kansas. Records indicated that they were living in Virgil upon enlistment. William "C." Hatley from Greenville, Kansas served in the 16th Kansas Cavalry Regiment but could not be confirmed as a blood relation.

The Hatley brothers served under the Army of the Frontiers' 1st Division Commanding Officer Major General James G. Blunt according to the official Report of the Adjutant General of the State of Kansas, Volume 1, 1861-1865. The Hatleys' service as dragoons with the 9th Kansas revealed specialized skills handling horses. Sam Hatley, my first-generation grandfather, had inherited his love of training mounts and driving cattle no doubt from his father. I never knew Sam or Leroy 'but their blood ran through my veins like the Oklahoma rains.'

At some point in the 1930s, Sam had traveled into Arkansas and Missouri playing the fiddle. Enlisted on July 1, 1863, Leroy and his brothers served two years and sixteen days with the Union cavalry responding to Cherokee raiding led by General Watie and Colonel Adair. Units of the Ninth had participated in five battles during the deadly era of Civil War: Battle of Dry Wood Creek 1861, Battle of Newtonia I, Cane Hill, and Prairie Grove 1862 to include the Battle of Baxter Springs 1863 (Civil War Soldiers, 2015). Most of Mike Company mustered out at Devall's Bluff, Arkansas in July 1865 following Lee's surrender in April.

Combat exposure affected people in different ways. Some soldiers encountered mental injuries while others dealt with physical depletion. War may have taken place in different parts of the globe but war in and of itself remained a violent event and so goes the witnessing of such. Often battles never ended for returning soldiers. The same was true then as it was today.

Shortly after the Civil War, Leroy Hatley found himself in State Hospital Number 3 located in Nevada, Missouri. Unofficial sources indicated that my great grandfather died of epilepsy, a disorder of the brain marked by repeated seizures. I disagreed with the diagnosis and maintained that perhaps an infectious agent may have been at work. To be honest, pathogenic disease effected Union and Confederate soldiers in surreal ways. Measles, mumps, dysentery and other camp diseases "constantly sniped at command numbers" (Davis, 1981, p. 133). Infection ran through units like the Black Death.

Evidenced in the archives, commanders regularly replaced and consolidated units because of disease. Wounded soldiers frequently had to fight off parenteral routed microorganisms in the form of gangrene. Private William Hatley, who had served in Clagett's Company with Leroy and Sherrod, died while on active duty in 1864. According to the Adjutant General's information on the Ninth Regiment Volunteers Cavalry, William tragically passed away on April 21 shortly after having contracted a virus.

While we tended to praise the heroes that survived, we equally mourned for those souls taken from us by the ravages of combat (See A Departed Brother). Family-wise, William Hatley turned out to be my great uncle. The cause of death, according to the war diary, had been due to a measles outbreak in his company. Accordingly, Mike Company had the most battlefield deaths from bacterial disease (29/129=22%) as compared with the rest of the regiment.

Illnesses rampaged the enlistees and officers equally. Edmund Kirby Smith, who had served as a general for the Confederacy, had been stricken with 10 days of dysentery but survived (Cornell University & U. S. War Department, 1902, p. 26). A cholera outbreak had been experienced in United States Colored Troops' (USCT) regiments. Private William Hatley had not been found buried at Oak Grove Cemetery.

Unfortunately, I knew only shorts about Private Sherrod Hatley. In the document Union Defenders of Kansas 1865 Greenwood County, I noticed that Sherrod looked to be five years older than his brother Leroy at the time of enlistment. The men's father also carried the name Sherod Hatley and had been listed as head-of-household. From the investigation on the son, what stood out had been the father's heritage from Hardin County, Tennessee where I found ties to Sarah Amanda Richards Hatley (1825-1904), a great grandmother. She had been discussed in the Missouri Gravestones Project No. 810327 along with my grandfather, Private Leroy Hatley No. 803788.

I noted the discovery of Mark Marcus Hatley who looked to be a veteran of the War of 1812 and who I believed shared a family branch in the Hatley tree. An even stronger relationship appeared with John Hatley Sr. who appeared to be a Revolutionary War veteran, another ghost of war, another great grandfather, and probably the hero of another book.

Cavalrymen stationed in Kansas had been tasked at bringing peace to a region that showed little faith in the promises of a government that could not be trusted by words or paper. Outgunned and outnumbered, the Cherokee ransacked relentlessly. As it played out historically, there had been a good chance that the Hatley's engaged forces loyal to Quantrill and General Watie. The general's units constantly harassed and blocked supply lines extending from Fort Scott, Kansas south to Fort Gibson, Oklahoma. Missouri war records noted the following set of Hatley soldiers who fought in the Civil War (MDH, 2015b):

Second Corporal D. Hatley	Kilo Company, 6th Missouri Volunteer Infantry, enlisted in March 1863 at Pocahontas, Arkansas.
Private Henderson Hatley	Kilo Company, 6th Missouri Volunteer Infantry, enlisted in March 1862 at Pocahontas, Arkansas; fought in the Battle of Forts Pillow, Iuka, Gibson, Baker's Creek, and at Vicksburg; he

went across the Mississippi River after the fall of Vicksburg.

Private John Hatley

India Company, Clark's Regiment Missouri Infantry, enlisted in 1862 at Fort Gibson, Oklahoma; believed to have become a Prisoner of War.

Private Presley Hatley

Kilo Company, 6th Missouri Volunteer Infantry, enlisted in March 1862 at Pocahontas, Arkansas; fought in the Battle of Fort Pillow, Iuka, Corinth, and Vicksburg; went across the Mississippi River after the fall of Vicksburg.

Private J. M. Hatley

Charlie Company, 1st Battalion Missouri Infantry, enlisted in February 1862 at Clarkton, Missouri; had been listed as absent without leave four months later in June 1862.

Private William C. Hatley

Bravo Company, 39th Regiment, enlisted in September 1862 at Parkville, Missouri.

It just so happened that all of these Hatley warriors had served on the side of the Confederacy. Union brass and President Lincoln felt that Vicksburg would be the key to winning the war. As illustrated in the Missouri combat record, Lieutenant General John Pemberton's Confederate defeat and ultimate surrender on July 4, 1863 at Vicksburg to the Union Army (Foner, 2006) sent many of his 30,000-man army scattering across the Mississippi River. Some Rebels managed to escape while others had not been so propitious. Hatley's could be found among those captured.

Strategically, the Union victory at Vicksburg changed the momentum in the Civil War. The Union could now control the Mississippi River. Vicksburg divided the Confederacy like never before and yet, the Rebels refused to abdicate. In the West, the Cherokee continued to battle on horseback. I distinctly found it odd that the Cherokee named their children after war heroes and politicians while at the same time experiencing rampant degradation. The Adair's had a standing tradition of beating the odds through honor and sacrifice.

Privates Virgil Balentine Adair and George Washington Adair VI

Although not genetically related, the Adair and Hatley families shared distinctive parts of their lives together which included the Oak Grove Cemetery in Stilwell, Oklahoma. Both families offered up men and women to serve during the Civil War. The don't-blink-or-you'll miss-it small Oak Grove community had been established after the War of 1812 but prior to the war between the States. The Adair's founded the community cemetery in 1838 according to the Indian-Pioneer History Project underwritten by W.J.B. Bigby, 1937.

The family of Adair's I knew belonged to the same genetic tree of Cherokee Principal Chief John Ross and Private Virgil Balentine Adair (1842-1910). Known as Balentine by his ancestors, the private's father appeared to be John Ross Adair buried at Chalk Bluff Cemetery located on the western side of the Evansville Creek.

Before he passed, I had the distinguished pleasure of visiting and discussing the old times with Jess E. Adair, grandson of Balentine. At the time, I had not thought about writing a second book. Our conversations proved to be genuine. We talked briefly about his ancestors but saved most of our banters about life and happy times. I soon realized after Jess died that we had been on a journey together, one that was sure to wake up some spirits. Never once did my friend ever speak Cherokee in front of me. One day we shall meet again, 'when the wolf and deer make tracks down the snowy mountain.'

According to his great grandson, the Honorable Mr. Larry Adair, former Oklahoma State Speaker of the House of Representatives and Vietnam Veteran, Balentine Adair had served in a Confederate unit from Georgia during the Civil War (Personal Communication, May 21, 2017). The intelligence on Private Adair showed him to be attached to Alpha Company 39th Georgia Volunteer Infantry Regiment, an outfit that formed in Murray County, Georgia in the spring of 1862 (murraycountymuseum.com, 2017). Balentine's company had also been referred to as the Cohutta Rangers (murraycountymuseum.com, 2017).

According to Henderson's (1960) Roster of the Confederate Soldiers of Georgia 1861- 1865, Balentine enlisted on March 10, 1862, had been captured one year and four months later on July 4, 1863 at Vicksburg, and appeared for the last time on the company roll October 31, 1863. After his service period, he returned home to Adairsville, Georgia.

As told to me by Larry Adair, Balentine's family migrated by wagon from Adairsville, Georgia to the Goingsnake District in Oklahoma in 1868 (Personal Communication, May 21, 2017). Adair roots had become fractured by Indian Removal and war. The move reunited the Adair's at Oak Grove. The grave of Balentine Adair could be found within hiking distance of Oak Grove at the Piney Cemetery where at one time, the Adair's operated a timber mill that fit the needs of Eastern Oklahoma and Western Arkansas. On Adair's gravestone at Piney had been chiseled the phrase, "In my father's house are many mansions." The Adair's were rightly heroes in the American journey.

History on the Cohutta Rangers traced back to the American Revolution and War of 1812. To see them come of age in the Civil

War seemed unsurprising. The Cohutta Rangers mustered as an elite unit skilled in weapons, horses, and explosives and performed missions similar to the Cherokee mounted rifle units. Cumulatively, 155 Rangers could be found on Adair's company roster, the majority of which enlisted with Adair (murraycountymuseum.com, 2017). With little time to train, two months later the Rangers found themselves in combat fighting for their young lives. Adair experienced scenes of bloodshed in the Vicksburg Campaign and the Battle of Bakers Creek also discussed as Champion Hill.

President Lincoln echoed the sentiments of his opposite, Jefferson Davis: To take or lose Vicksburg would be the key to victory or capitulation. Both men understood the value of the Mississippi River and the ports that snaked around Vicksburg. Initially, General's Sherman and Grant failed to successfully attack Vicksburg from the Northwest and Northeast. Physical barriers halted their advance. Books and documents showed that Union forces struggled to contend with the swamps of Louisiana and Mississippi.

Vicksburg stood as an impenetrable fortress to the North and West protected by the Mississippi River and its tributaries but vulnerable in the East. Private Adair's regiment supported a perimeter guarded by seasoned Confederate infantrymen and an artillery commander trained at West Point by the name of John Clifford Pemberton. Ultimately, Pemberton's mission to defend Vicksburg would be in vain:

> Despite constant pleas to [General Joseph E.] Johnston for aid, Pemberton was completely isolated. Eventually, a lack of supplies and starvation [took] their toll. On July 4, 1863 after 46 days, Pemberton surrendered 2,166 officers and 27,230 men, 172 cannon, and almost 60,000 muskets and rifles to the Federals (Civil War Trust, 2017).

Fighting at Antietam in the fall of 1862 had been costly for both sides. With his gonads in jeopardy, Ulysses Grant needed a win at Vicksburg and he got it. The summer of 1863 turned into a bloodbath. At least 8, 000 men had been KIA by July 4 with thousands wounded and diseased. Following capitulation and while captured, Balentine and several Cohutta Rangers underwent federal detainment and interrogation. Eventually their captors offered Adair and the men options with parole. Some of the soldiers changed sides and took oaths of service with the Yankees.

One of the first things that I noticed about the Ranger Company focused on just the numbers: I counted 27 men captured (17%) during the Vicksburg Campaign; approximately four men had been KIA, two of which may have been brothers (Privates John and Joseph Henderson) who died on the same day at Baker's Creek; desertion and absent without leave figures showed to be elevated in the company, where at minimum five non-commissioned officers and 26 privates had disappeared; several members of the company were killed or captured in other battles or died of disease. Union recruiting appeared strong because the record revealed that men had been captured and squeezed to turn coat. I admired the fact that after his capture, Balentine chose to return home instead of dishonoring himself by becoming a Yankee.

I was unsure that I had been able to connect Balentine and the Adair's my family had been acquainted with in relation to Private George Washington Adair VI. Surely, I had to be close since members from each family had been buried in the same cemeteries in or around Oak Grove. Quickly, I found myself juggling six generations of George's that became sons, farmers, soldiers, husbands, brothers, and cousins.

Data surfaced on a George Adair VI who had served with the Confederate Second Cherokee Mounted Rifles. I needed to confirm this militarily. The problems I encountered with George VI centered on patronymics and surnamed-name chains. In documents, recorders sometimes failed to denote successive generations like "VI."

It seemed hard to go wrong with the name George Washington preceding one's surname. Heck! We had one or two in my own family. Still considered America's greatest executive, President George Washington had quite the following in successive generations of Cherokee citizens. In one example, Chief Ross had a son named George Washington Ross who served in the Indian Home Guard during the Civil War. Gaines (1989) recognized him as a Lieutenant in Hotel Company in Colonel John Drew's Regiment during the Pea Ridge Campaign (p. 151). In another instance, I discovered a Colonel George Washington Adair who had served the Confederacy under General Nathan Bedford Forrest.

Eventually, I found my target. Private George Washington Adair VI (1837-1870) was revealed to be the Cherokee regimental soldier from Stilwell who fought in the Civil War, who died at the young age of 32, and who occupied a burial plot in the Oak Grove Cemetery with my ancestors. George VI had been born in Georgia following Removal but had died in Oklahoma. The age and year of his death raised questions for me.

My work on Private Adair yielded an understanding of how the Adair family residents of Oak Grove on the Evansville Creek and specifically the marriage of Samuel Houston Adair and Sarah Stapler Ross connected to the Chief Ross family buried at Parkhill Cemetery in Cherokee County near Tahlequah. It also revealed the fact that some Adair family members migrated from Georgia to Texas and then to Oklahoma. Samuel Houston Adair had been born in Texas. Historically, Chief Ross had served with General Sam Houston at the Battle of Horseshoe Bend. My grandfather Sam Hatley and Sam Adair would have been acquaintances at Oak Grove.

Father of Sam Adair, Judge John Thompson Adair established the Oak Grove Cemetery of Stilwell around 1838. George Adair VI's parents showed to be Calvin Sequoyah Adair who died at a middle age of 48 years and Lucy Starr both sited in Oak Grove Cemetery. Born in traditional Cherokee lands, Private Adair was one of 38 other Adair's buried at Oak Grove. At Piney Cemetery nearby, 40 Adair's declared gravesites. At Chalk Bluff Cemetery a mile west of Oak Grove, only four Adair's could be found. Through the Judge's efforts and foresight, Stilwell became the Adair family's second home.

Private Adair VI had served in Kilo Company Second Regiment Cherokee Mounted Rifles according to Find-a-Grave contributor, TS Lundberg Nee Sternburg. Adair looked to be about 24 years old when the Confederate Navy relentlessly shelled Fort Sumpter. He joined the fight in Indian Territory, Oklahoma. Skirmishing and raiding the Federals, in September 1864, Private Adair's unit battled at Cabin Creek but later surrendered at Doaksville (Lundberg Nee Sternburg, 2010) in the Choctaw Nation. I had also encountered textual information which stipulated that George Adair VI served in the Battle of Pea Ridge Arkansas. I looked for confirmation but easily got sidetracked by another G.W. Adair and for good reason.

The Cherokee Registry listed an older George Washington Adair II (b. 1806) as one of Stand Watie's first commissary officers, but no rank had been specified (Cherokee Heritage Documentation Center, 2015). The George Washington Adair that had served as a commissary officer was the same Adair that had accompanied the Treaty Party to Washington D.C. for the Treaty of 1846 and an original signer of the New Echota Treaty in 1835. To be clear, this was not the George Adair buried at Oak Grove.

Adair II became a reminder of how intensely the Cherokee Nation remained split over political power and New Echota. It showed itself in how the mounted rifles regiments would eventually be arranged. Interred at the Ross-Mayes Cemetery, Adair II was the father of Colonel William Penn Adair, Civil War officer and lawyer by profession, who helped establish the Cherokee in Rusk County, Texas. William Adair became a voice for the Ridge Party in its contentiousness with Ross allies and why he became a leader and member of the Second Regiment.

According to Lundberg Nee Sternburg (2010), Colonel William Adair had served as one of Private Adair VI's field officers in the Second Regiment which meant that his commanding officer had been Stand Watie, a colonel at the time. Gaines (1989) reported that following the Tahlequah Council's meeting when the Cherokee Nation collectively decided to ally with the Confederacy, Colonel Drew would lead the regiment loyal to the Ross' while Watie would manage the regiment spirited by Ridge supporters (p. 13-15). Even though the Nation openly appeared politically divided, the brigade formed nonetheless and General Albert Pike rode the Indian soldiers into Arkansas (Civil War Trust, 2018).

An excerpt from the Pea Ridge affair noted the following: Prior to battle, "Pike's Indian Brigade had about 1,000 soldiers which included a unit of Texas cavalry" (U.S. National Park Service). As well, the Indian Brigade's activities at Pea Ridge became recognized with scrutiny "when a number of Federal dead were found scalped and mutilated" (NPS). The Indian Brigade stood accused of the atrocity resulting in General Pike being vigorously denounced throughout the North (NPS). Civil War Trust (2018) confirmed that the event took place on Foster's Farm.

It became my opinion that George VI had not participated in the scalping but no proof either way could be offered at present. To be frank, I despised the white man's protocols for war anyway. Did combat truly operate on a set of rules? What's fair in killing or being killed? What levels of revenge might be appropriate? Furthermore, scalping did not originate in the tribes of American Indians. The method had been started by Europeans intending to divide the Indian Nations. What I could verify with specificity was that Private George Washington Adair VI had been buried in the same cemetery with his first sergeant, Mark Bean (Lundberg Nee Sternburg, 2010). At the end of the work on Adair VI, I gathered the perception that Oak Grove had become a cemetery of Adair's who supported Stand Watie and Major Ridge. This explained why some Adair's moved on to Tahlequah while others remained in Stilwell.

Chief Lewis Downing

A bevy of full-blooded and mix-blooded Cherokee families became personally affected by war and internal political conflict. Located in Mayes County, Oklahoma, the cemetery in Murphy held the remains of skilled political and military leader of the Cherokee Nation, the Honorable Chief Lewis Downing (1821-1872). The Downing's shared a cemetery with Adair's at Haner. The highly respected chief appeared unique in that he had served in both the Confederacy and the Union during the Civil War. As a study, Chief Downing represented the Tennessee lines of Cherokee descent (See IMG4).

A reliable visionary, Chief Downing believed that the best path for his people would be compromise between the mixed and full-blooded Cherokee. Combat and treaty revenge stood in his way. During the Civil War, the gracious chaplain had been assigned to the First Regiment of the Cherokee Mounted Rifles from October 1861 to July 1862. After watching men die in horrific ways, the chief made a big decision: Downing turned coat over the issue of slavery, although he had practiced slavery himself, and volunteered to serve for the cause of the Federals.

Downing's decision placed him at odds with Stand Watie and other Cherokee factions which disfavored abolitionism. This would not be the first time in their illustrious history that the Cherokee would do battle against each other or the United States Government. Chief Downing looked to be a valiant leader in a long list of heroes like Moytoy of Tellico, Dragging Canoe, Little Turkey, Black Fox, and Pathkiller.

Military leaders bragged about their fighting Native American regiments. Pea Ridge was the first sizable battle of the Civil War to involve Indian troops, mostly because their current homeland lay only a few miles West of the battlefield (Civil War Trust, 2018). I expected to find Chief Downing on the Pea Ridge battle roster. Interestingly, the good chief became a social builder from the pulpit. His efforts would one day help reunify the Nation in Oklahoma.

When the Civil War broke out, Chief John Ross and his family headed back East out of concern over Confederate reprisals in Indian Territory. Chief Downing became the Acting Principal Chief of the Cherokee Nation but his thunder had been immediately suppressed by Stand Watie who had received the majority of the vote during the 1862 Cherokee Election replacing Chief Ross. According to Franks writing for the Oklahoma Historical Society, Watie became the life-long enemy of Ross (2009, para. 4). Watie's distaste for Downing proved to be contrived merely by association.

Political problems continued to swirl in the Cherokee Nation after the war. Private Adair VI returned home to an uncertain future. One year following Lee's surrender to Grant, Chief Ross suddenly died in Washington while trying to negotiate a new agreement for the Cherokee (Thoborn, 1924, p. 142). Following his death, Colonel William Potter Ross temporarily served as Principal Custodian before Chief Downing took the post (Anderson, 2009). Ironically, Colonel

Ross replaced Chief Downing when he died during his second term (Anderson, 2009).

In 1867, the Cherokee finalized a new treaty whereby securing the whole of the Nation. Lewis Downing's Party came to power as a result. Thoborn recorded in 1924 that a compromise had been reached between the Cherokee party factions, Loyalists versus the Treaty Party, thus "ending the carnival of violence and bloodshed where peace and prosperity came back to the Cherokee Nation" (p. 145). The Cherokee had not seen fervent peace since the 1700s. Unfortunately, concordance would last only a few years.

Sergeant W.H. Collins

Who was Sergeant W.H. Collins? The surname alone garnered population density in many U.S. states. Little did I know that it would be the "W.H." that would end up causing so much confusion. Male soldiers named W.H. Collins could be found in the War of the Rebellion on both sides with a few carrying a non-commissioned officers rank. Several W.H. Collins' had served in the U.S. Armed Forces going all the way back to the American Revolution. The Civil War in America was unique in that for the first time American families would send fathers and sons off to fight a war against other Americans. Opposed, the Collins families suffered tremendously and carried their fair share of war-dead.

In my family, Great Uncle James Collins who had served in WWI looked to be quite handsome in his military uniform. Like the Adair's, Hatley's, Garrett's, and Riden's, the Collins' battled each other from time to time. The river-land battle for Vicksburg was no exception. Weighted by a heavy barrage of candidates and casualties, I set out to find Sergeant W.H. Collins' war ghost. The search for Sergeant Collins revealed once again that the Collins trees originated from warriors, disciplined and decorated men of the horse, sword and rifle.

According to a digitized Medical Certificate of Disability provided by the Missouri History Museum (2009), a Sergeant W.H. Collins had served in Alpha Company's Second and Sixth Missouri Infantry Regiments attached to Cockrell's Brigade in the Army of Tennessee. Visible from a document dated August 10, 1864, physicians at the Civil War hospital in Uniontown, Alabama determined Collins to be "unfit for military duty" due to "a gunshot wound to the left leg" and that the injury had become complicated because of the onset of gangrene (Missouri History Museum, 2009).

Collins' health had become so severe that he could not travel for thirty days (Missouri History Museum, 2009). The record did not stipulate which battle that Collins had participated in to have received his ailment.

Historians praised the actions of the Second Missouri Infantry during the Civil War. By April 1863, Brigadier General Marion Cockrell had taken command of the newly reorganized Second and Sixth Infantry attached to the First Missouri Brigade. Within a short period of time, the general had turned the units into victorious fighters. A Missourian at birth, General Cockrell began his career as a young captain in the Missouri State Guard like my great grandfather Captain William Charles Riden, both having served under General Sterling Price.

A host of soldiers named Collins fought and died on the soil of Vicksburg, Mississippi. Upon searching the parole and confinement rosters from Vicksburg, I found fifty-eight Confederate records bearing the Collins surname (U.S. National Park Service, Vicksburg National Military Park). None had detailed the services of a sergeant by the name of W.H. Collins with the Second or Sixth Missouri Infantry. I did discover a W.H.H. Collins with the Second but he had served in a different company (USNPS, VNMP, 2016).

Of the Collins graves buried in the national cemetery, five men had died on site during the siege or shortly afterwards. Sergeant W.H. Collins' name never appeared on any parole or confinement record or even a death plot. For some strange reason however, the 1864 medical examination claimed not only that he was a "patient" but also an "inmate" (Missouri History Museum, 2009). Therefore, I rolled with the inkling that at Vicksburg, he had been shot, captured, and ultimately incarcerated.

Given the information, I considered the notion that W.H. Collins had fought at Vicksburg with Alpha Company and survived. I confirmed that the Second Missouri did indeed participate in the actions at Vicksburg (USNPS, VNMP, 2016). Unfortunately, if Sergeant Collins battled at Vicksburg and had been wounded and captured, his personal data never appeared in any of the park's disposition files.

First Brigade and the 2nd-6th Missouri saw action at Kennesaw Mountain, Georgia and the Atlanta campaign with particular heroism at the Battle of Altoona Pass and Franklin, Tennessee (2ndmissouri.com, 2015). In the Battle of Franklin, Cockrell's valiant assault on the Union fell short where he lost 60.2% of his force (2ndmissouri.com, 2015). Fighting at Altoona Pass had occurred in October 1864 and at Franklin in November 1864. Sergeant Collins had been wounded before August 1864. Therefore, he could not have taken part in these battles. Because the Battle of Kennesaw Mountain had been fought on June 27, it seemed possible that Sergeant W.H. Collins received his wound in this earlier engagement.

Collins' fate changed sometime after the summer of 1863 but before the engagement at Altoona Pass. His discharge had been approved one year after Vicksburg. On page two, the disability certificate showed that Collins had been transferred from Gamble Hospital in Georgia where he had received a thirty-day furlough on July 12, 1864 (Missouri History Museum, 2009). As a circumstance of being wounded, I noted the Uniontown doctor's mention that Collins suffered specifically from "bifurcation of gangrene" (Missouri History Museum, 2009).

As a disease, gangrene had a rapid incubation period with signs appearing after about eight hours. To say that his leg had become bifurcated meant the gangrene had spread which in turn signaled that a time element was involved in the injury. For these purposes, I found it probable that Sergeant Collins had been shot in the leg at Kennesaw

Mountain. That injury would have been debilitating because the doctors in Uniontown found Collins to be in "generally bad health" (Missouri History Museum, 2009). Following Kennesaw, fifteen days would have passed before he received the furlough thus allowing for the gangrene to replicate.

Certainly curious, I looked at the role of Gamble Hospital during the Civil War and found myself in Newnan, Georgia in front of a roster of medical doctors that serviced the needs of Confederate injured. I ran across the name, Samuel H. Stout Army Medical Director of the Army of Tennessee. Immediately returning to Sergeant Collins' disability certificate, I verified the by direction signature of Dr. Stout (Missouri History Museum, 2009).

A huge problem remained in Sergeant Collins' biography: If Collins had served in the First Brigade commanded by General Cockrell, a Confederate outfit, then why was he an inmate in a Confederate hospital? This question became the 'elephant in the room. Thinking his gravesite might offer clues, his interment was never discovered. Consequentially, I could not corroborate his standing in the Collins-Hatley family tree. And while Missouri as a state connected me to Sergeant Collins, admittedly I had failed to establish a genetic link between us.

After receiving new orders to the East Coast, I visited the Vicksburg battle grounds on my way to Camp Lejeune in early summer, 1996. The bearing of the Missouri troops had won from General Pemberton, as it did from all others, the highest encomiums. Even in defeat, the austere commanding officer expressed praise for his brave soldiers of the 1st Brigade: "that if he had ten thousand Missourians, he would have cut his way out [of the Vicksburg Siege] rather than surrender" (Anderson, 1868, p. 356). Historically, more than 75 Medals of Honor had been awarded to Missouri combat veterans.

Missouri war records noted the following information on Collins soldiers that fought with the Union and Confederacy in the Civil War: I calculated that approximately 560 Oath's of Enlistment had been taken (MDH, 2015c). In a sample population of servicemen, Union soldiers outnumbered Confederate soldiers eight men against two men (8:2 ratio). Many Collins family members answered the call to duty despite an overwhelming propensity to battle blood kin.

A dangerous occupation indeed, being a soldier paid hideously. Private R.A. Collins, who had obliged Bledsoe's Confederate Artillery for six months, earned $90 which equated to $15 per month. Poorly compensated, soldiers suffered tremendous hardships while on duty.

Enlisted at Warrensburg, Missouri on January 29, 1862, hard-charger Confederate James E. Collins of Hotel Company Second Missouri Infantry Regiment had just been promoted to the rank of sergeant. Following wounds received in the Siege of Corinth, the sergeant died of combat-related health complications less than a year later. Soldiering became a precarious job with few positives and high rates of death.

To be successful at Vicksburg, Grant needed Corinth and he took it as the Confederates withdrew. Because he grew up a northerner, Grant failed to anticipate the values of loyalty and patriotism that he would face at Vicksburg. One month before the siege began on May 10, 1863, Private Charles Collins enlisted to fight for the Confederacy in Bovine, Mississippi. While serving with Echo Company 2nd Missouri Infantry Regiment, he was KIA when his parapet was blown up. By example, Private Collins had served and died in a short period of time, thus reinforcing one's previously contrived notion that many men served in combat with little or no training.

At the age of 33, Union soldier Private Owen Collins from St. Joseph, Missouri served with Golf Company 51st Infantry Regiment. Tragically, he died of smallpox five weeks after his enlistment. Private

D.J. Collins of Bravo Company and other Missourians had served with the Confederate Army's 1st Arkansas Cavalry. Like so many unfortunate souls, D.J. was one of 32 other prisoners that died in 1864 while incarcerated at the smallpox-ridden military prison in Little Rock, Arkansas. Early in the war, Arkansas saw itself siding with the CSA until 1863 when Little Rock fell to Union forces.

Hatley and Collins ancestry had evolved throughout Arkansas, Tennessee, and the South. The First, Fourth, and Sixth Arkansas Infantry had seen action with Major General Braxton. More than twenty Collins' from Missouri and Arkansas had served with the Union's United States Colored Troops (USCT) infantry regiments during the Civil War (Missouri Digital Heritage, 2015). I found it shameful that so much of Black History had been missed by modern scholars. Of the records I analyzed, several things stood out on the Regimental USCT Infantry Cards, Form No. 241g A.G.O. 1-28-10 (MDH, 2015c):

With a sample size of N=23, the data showed that men serving under the surname Collins had fought and died for their country just like white men. Two soldiers had been promoted to corporal during their period of service. Although age had been missed on most of the cards, soldiers as young as 18 and as old as 33 were noted. The regimental cards did not list the battles each soldier had fought in, but from the limited notes available, it became clear to me that the 18th, 56th, 60th, 62nd, 65th, 67th, and 68th Regiments had seen more than their fair share of combat. Out of the original 23 soldiers who had first mustered at Benton Barracks in St. Louis, 12 infantrymen had been KIA or had later died from their wounds or disease in a Baton Rouge, Louisiana hospital.

The USCT had served their country with honor. They died for the cause of freedom which would not fully arrive for 100 years. Only a handful of soldiers of the Missouri USCT units had been born when the Missouri Compromise had been agreed upon in 1820. The idea of slavery flourishing in Missouri ultimately failed but it took a full generation later to come to grips with its torments and contend against its evils. When Lincoln signed the Emancipation Proclamation in 1863, military service presented the USCT with purpose.

Escaped slaves from South Carolina and Florida collectively became the first slave regiment mustered into Union service, recognized by Higginson and Gray to be the First South Carolina Volunteers (1970, p. 3).

The Collins' who served in the USCT regiments of Missouri understood their mission and they volunteered for certain death based on the belief that one day their children and their children's children would live in a World free of racism and oppression. Date analysis on the 23 Missouri soldiers of USCT regiments showed that a high frequency of enlistments occurred in 1863 and continued through 1864 (Missouri Digital, 2015).

The largest trees of Collins' serving in the Union Army came out of New York. In archived digital records available from the New York State Military Museum and Veterans Research Center (NYSMM & VRC), soldiers with the surname Collins proved to be unbelievably extensive. The site featured 194 infantry regiments, an independent battalion of light infantry, 26 cavalry regiments, the Oneida Independent Cavalry Company, three regiments of engineers, one battalion of sharpshooters, 34 artillery firing batteries, and additional units of marine artillery (NYSMM & VRC, 2015). I became reminded of the ghost of General Duke who commanded Collins' loyal to the Confederacy.

General Basil Duke

Confederate raider of Indiana and Ohio; leader and tactical commander of elite soldiers in Missouri and Kentucky; brilliant officer serving under the command of legendary Brigadier General John Hunt Morgan; a man of integrity guided by the principles of order and fairness. These character traits had been used over the years to describe the dossier of General Basil Duke (1838-1916). Few southerners displayed the unique qualifications that Duke possessed.

Some Confederate officers had law degrees and Basil appeared to be one of them. Apparently the counselor was practicing in Missouri when he became the leader of a pro-Southern faction in St. Louis known as the Minute Men (mocivilwar.org, 2015). Borrowed from the pages of the American Revolution, they positioned themselves as paramilitary secessionists and responded to insurrection by fire and maneuver.

I looked at the famous officer hopeful of grasping how influential he may have been in Central Missouri and if my ancestors knew of him or had served in complimentary units. I also sought to bring to finality the naming of Duke, Missouri close to where my family had land and a cave. General Duke had spent time in the Missouri State Guard around the same time frame when my great grandfather obliged General Price. When I investigated Duke, I hoped to find notes about Captain William Charles Riden. That attempt never came to fruition.

A graduate of Transylvania University Law, the Civil War forced Duke to put his legal aspirations on hold. Like so many young people whose fathers and ancestors had fought bravely in the American Revolution and War of 1812, Duke became caught up in the hostilities of the John Brown-Bleeding Kansas Affair. With not a lot of reflection, Duke immediately turned to the leadership of the Confederacy.

Believed to have been wounded several times, Duke had served in the Civil War from start to finish. He may have been the luckiest officer in the Confederate Army. What made General Duke special appeared to be his ability to teach his raider's tactical strategy, something all great military soldiers did well. General Duke's ghost could walk the halls of Patton and MacArthur. General Duke surrendered after Lee's conditionals at Appomattox but did so before Cherokee leader, Stand Watie.

General Duke looked to be arguably one of the most talented officers the C.S.A. had in its ranks. In his post-war intellectual days, the general had gained acclaim as a published author. Military data showed that Duke had served as Morgan's Executive Officer throughout Kentucky, Tennessee, Ohio, Indiana, and West Virginia. Late in his career, the astute general may have even served as a bodyguard to Confederate President Jefferson Davis.

It was my understanding that General Duke had been captured at the Battle of Buffington Island in July of 1863 but took command of Morgan's Raiders after its commanding officer had been killed in September 1864. Much had been written about Duke's services to Morgan. Both men could be found buried with their families in Lexington, Kentucky.

I looked extensively at the naming of Duke, Missouri trying to uncover any kind of factual evidence or community connection with the astute general. Clarifying the naming of the town Duke turned out to be simple and discoverable through the State Historical Society of Missouri: Duke was named for the popular smoking tobacco called "Duke's Mixture." It had nothing to do with General Duke. Thus, my thoughts had been easily corrected.

Two years of research had not yielded an extensive amount of material on the general's exploits in Missouri. I had read pieces of secondary information inferring that General Duke had been involved in planning the destruction of the Osage River Bridge. On point, my eyes perked up because General Duke may have been connected with something my great uncle had been arrested and killed for. I guessed even lawyers got their hands dirty.

Captain (John) Wesley Riden

How in the timber fields of Missouri did a justice's son and grandchild turn up dead along the side of a road in Southwest Missouri at a place called McCortney Hollow? How was it even possible that the progeny of a Valley Forge survivor and nephew of a state pioneer and community leader get blasted at point-blank range by cannon? The murders and burials would always be a mystery. Until now, the deaths had been forgotten thus revealing that Captain (John) Wesley Riden and his children became ghosts of war, something Owen 1912 had predicted (See The Unreturning).

Eyewitness accounts murmured that Captain Wesley Riden and his two newborn twins had died at the hands of Union soldiers on March 1, 1864. Although tentatively the exact facts remained unclear, my intuition reigned in favor of the idea that my kinfolk had been directly sought out, or at least the captain had. Currently I conceded, if only in a limited capacity, to the consideration that bushwhackers through happenstance killed the Riden's. Captain Riden had been seen and subsequently arrested for speaking out against the Union. The lesson: "Never draw fire --- it irritates everyone around you" (USMCRP, Rule 3, 1992).

By August 1862, Captain Riden had been detained twice and taken to Rolla, Missouri. The Provost's Office and Federals knew the guardsman because they were familiar with his brother and my great grandfather, also a well-known captain in the Missouri State Guard. Officers who fought in the Civil War came from a variety of backgrounds including medicine, mercantilism, religion, and farming. My uncle's past showed that he was an honest person and civic business leader. In as much, Wesley Riden positioned himself as a man like his father, Joseph Warren Riden Sr., a farmer and judge with an impeccable reputation.

Quite a few officers in service to both armies practiced law as civilians. To blame the carnage in Kansas and Missouri simply on a legal fight over abolitionism or the 1857 Dred Scott decision seemed unlikely. According to the rights of man, what legality had Wesley Riden violated? Lines between right and wrong became blurred by what he might have said in public. Was it not freedom of expression that in part motivated American Patriots to rebel against King George III? Silencing my great uncle may have been politically motivated but his death and those of my infant cousins portrayed a triple homicide.

Generally, shenanigans would not get one killed. The Riden families had an extensive farming operation in central and southwest Missouri counties including Dent, Phelps, Pulaski, Shannon, St. Francois, and Texas county. On one of their large farms near Duke close to the Big Piney River in Pulaski County, William Charles and Wesley had lived with their parents and extended family members. It seemed certainly possible that war may have divided the two brothers.

Hostilities forced the Riden's to choose so choose they did. The area where the Riden's called home, according to Primas, changed significantly because of the war: "Pulaski County depopulated by 1864 due to bushwhackers and the Union. Many families fled to Rolla where the Union Army had a big presence."

It became necessary to preview the Riden cases with legal advice on what constituted a crime. Expressing one's opinion should not have led to death given the community of real killers who pillaged and plundered Missouri during the Civil War. Conferring to common law, Cook's (1917) detailed studies published in Yale Law Review stipulated with conciseness the difference between and the collaboration of motive and intent:

Every crime may be looked at as composed of two elements: an act and the intention or state of mind with which the act was done. Did or did not the one who [performed] the act intend to bring about the results which actually took place? Was that his [or her] intention? Motive could be understood in terms of the reason or inducement to commit a malicious act...
(p. 646).

Given these two legal parameters, the question begged for lucidity: Who had broken the law? Wesley Riden or the Federals? Deceased children were involved. My sense became that Wesley probably found himself torn between his observation of governmental insurrection and how he felt about the rights of property and sovereignty, in a very literal sense these being the rights of man. The provost's office would remind him of who had the upper hand:

Good morning, the worm, your honor! The crown will plainly show the prisoner who stands before you was caught red-handed showing feelings, showing feelings of an almost human nature. This will not do... (Pink Floyd, The Trial)

In my dreams, I rode the midnight train to Gasconade and searched for the ghost of Wesley Riden. He was family. We shared blood.

As the research for this book evolved, one of its intentions turned to finding the grave locations of my uncle and cousins. Information from a secondary source had indicated that Wesley and at least one child were violently slain by Union troops near their home in Big Piney, Missouri. In 2009, M. Martin blogged about Captain Riden in a reply to a third party:

Riden was killed when Union soldiers came to his house and wanted money. He refused. They took him outside, tied him to a fence, and used him for target practice before shooting him

104

with cannon. His wife and children were made to watch (National Institute for Genealogy Studies-Genealogy Wise, 2015). Martin's annotation talked of the father being killed but not the children. Further evidentiary statements came to light:

Statement by James Riden:

Union soldiers came to his house and wanted money. He refused. They took him outside, tied him to a fence and used him for target practice before shooting him with a cannon. His wife and children were made to watch. [Riden's wife] Ellender had just had twins. One was bayonetted. She ran into the loft of the barn with the other and hid for days. The baby ended up dying (Hoy & Nail, 2017, No. 35).

Statement by Rachel Monroe:

In March of 1864, Union soldiers came to his house and demanded money. He refused to give them any; so, they took him outside - tied him to a fence and shot him before firing a cannon at him while his family watched. At some point during this, the soldiers also killed one of his month-old twin babies. His wife Ellender Cordella Huff ran off and hid in the loft of the barn for days with the other baby which also ended up dying (Hoy & Nail, 2017, No. 35).

Additional tidbits related to the deaths came from Fowke (2006, p. 57) in an article about archaeological findings from the Smithsonian Institute covering Riden's Cave. In 1864, the area where Wesley Riden and his family resided had appeared secluded. Professor Primas had told me "that the opening to Riden's cave was inconspicuous but the inside of the cave expansive." Inclined to accept the disposition that the Riden's had been struck down by a Union unit, it seemed possible that the cavalry encroaching on the Riden property had done so by happenstance.

If Wesley Riden thought for one second that Union soldiers were approaching, I felt like he would have taken his family into the cave. My impression therefore became that the Union force had caught the family by surprise. The National Institute for Genealogy Studies – Genealogy Wise (2015) had mentioned that Union soldiers were looking for money, which satisfied the element of motive.

It was my opinion that the Union soldiers who killed the Riden's did so with malice, like Calley's infantry squad at Pinkville or Custer's assault on the Southern Cheyenne along the banks of the Ouachita River. Blown-away by cannon, the killings seemed heartless where my uncle and his wife and kids never saw the danger coming. I began to feel more confident in the family assertion that all three graves were located in the Warren-McCortney Cemetery and the premise that they were buried close to where they had fallen. Judging from the grotesque manner in which they had been killed, burial would have been nasty and cumbersome.

What kind of man was Captain Wesley Riden? He was a gentleman of principle and integrity like his father and brother. His first marriage had been to a woman that had become pregnant by another man but widowed by a sudden death. Wesley previously owned land in Texas County and had entered into business agreements with local professionals. With a prominent elder involved in education and politics, one had to question why Wesley went rogue? That is to say, if going miscreant meant the freedom to speak or lack thereof.

Ultimately, the official burial site of my great uncle and cousins could not be confirmed. To be honest, I really had no official proof that two infant children had died because I had not visually found or inspected their death certificates. Fieldstones in the Warren-

McCortney Cemetery could have been easily displaced by flooding so close to the Big Piney River. Moreover, unless an exhumation could be performed proving that Wesley's body lay in the Burnett Cemetery as was rumored, the research had reached an impenetrable assumption: the bodies had been buried at Warren-McCortney.

Although my uncle was thought to be a Confederate soldier, no veteran-related stone of his could be found in the potential cemeteries in the area. Therefore, I could not rightly prove a murder case without a body but I was on point when I returned to a revamped interrogative: Who had the power to kill a justice's son and his grandchildren? I needed to dig deeper into the evidence.

Returning to the digital archives, I had been able to find a bundle of facts about the Collins', Garrett's, Riden's, Hatley's, and Adair's who had fought in the Civil War. The data appeared specific and detailed. Unfortunately, precise information on the full birth name John Wesley Riden appeared to be noticeably limited. In Missouri's Union Provost Marshal's Papers: 1861-1866, a "Wesley Riden" had been grouped with 13 other prisoners. I named the group the Rolla Fourteen. Wesley Riden's age at the time of his first arrest calculated to be 45 years old.

I could not help but wonder if Wesley Riden had been one of the soldiers from Price's MSG that had returned home for good after the Battle of Pea Ridge? Erwin wrote that many of the men who joined the MSG in 1861 "later became guerillas" (2012, p. 53). Wesley had joined the MSG several years before Pea Ridge so it seemed possible he could have turned guerilla. From his arrest record, we know that he disliked Union insurrection. The first arrest failed to change his mind. If he took an allegiance oath for the Union, he seemed to clearly be lying about it.

Discussion on the record claimed that the provost had taken Wesley Riden as a prisoner twice in 1862 "because of a plot to destroy a train near Gasconade, Missouri and for speaking out against the Union." In denoting the year 1862 as his incarceration period, Riden appeared to have been shot down by Union soldiers less than two years later or about twenty-nine days before his 46th birthday. The following showed Wesley Riden's provost record data:

Date:	6-5-1862
File No.	1088
City:	Rolla, Missouri
Charge:	Rumors of Planned Destruction of Train near Gasconade.
Penalty:	Take Oath of Allegiance on 6-30-1862

Date:	8-16-1862
File No.	Not provided
City:	Waynesville, Missouri
Charge:	Aiding the Rebellion by Speaking Words of Encouragement to Persons Engaged in Rebellion.
Penalty:	Not Disclosed

I would not classify Wesley Riden's murder as being KIA. His final penalty would be termed assassination for speaking out against political and military incursion. To find Wesley's reports, one needed to tool-up using his middle name rather than his first name in the search criteria. Unlike the records from Texas County which noted both Wesley's service and brother William Charles' in the MSG, archives never listed the former attached to a unit. His death had not been posted with other soldiers nor with other Riden burial lists. To say the least, I found it odd that he never appeared on any soldier burial list.

Founding pioneer of Missouri, Joseph Sr. had lost a son and I still needed to understand why. Wesley Riden's dual confinement in 1862 followed by his murder in 1864 pointed to him being militarily targeted, something that the eyewitnesses would not have known about.

At some point after Wesley's first detainment, which looked to be about 25 days, he had been released and had returned to his farm at Big Piney. During this time, the twins had been born. Clearly, the arrest marked him as a trouble maker in the eyes of local law officers and the Federals. It seemed relevant that Wesley Riden was being treated as a civilian agitator and not a military man because he had never been listed as POW.

Resources had listed Wesley Riden as a captain in the state guard. If the Federals had record of this, then it seemed quite conceivable that a mission to kill him could have been devised by Union leadership in Waynesville or Rolla. However, they would have also had to consider his community standing since he was a judge's son. The Union commanders in Rolla had grown frustrated because they had failed to control guerilla fighters in the southwest corridor. If the Union officers thought that my uncle was masterminding guerilla attacks and blowing up trains, they would have personally come after him. Thus, the savage means of killing him with cannon, if true, had been a planned ending.

The Union would have wanted to leave no doubt that he was dead. One must never be fooled into thinking that professionally trained officers do not commit brutal atrocities.

Being unsure of official grave sites for the Riden's was in keeping with how viciously Wesley Riden and his children had been rubbed out. Being shot with cannon would have left body parts everywhere (See IMG7). What would have remained to bury? The Riden's had been slain at some time during morning hours. Rumors about exploding the Gasconade train opened a door of inquiry: Could there be a bonfire connection between Riden and Gasconade?

Looking for summary data on the deaths, information was collected and analyzed from creditable work titled, Civil War Records for Gasconade, Maries, and Osage Counties: Extract from The War of the Rebellion: A Compilation of the Official Records of the Union and Confederate Armies available at Osage County.org (2015) and through Cornell University Library - United States War Department (1902). After reading the Union reports from the record and the communication transpiring being junior officers and senior officers, it appeared clear that Union military leaders had been greatly concerned about Confederate violence:

May 10, 1861	Confederate Brigadier General Basil Duke ordered the burning of the Osage River Bridge. Blowing the bridges slowed the advance of mechanized artillery and heavy equipment.
May 16, 1861	Confederate forces were reconnoitering train locomotives and cab cars for troop and weapons transport. Controlling the rivers and railroads were of utmost importance. On this date, General Duke stopped a small force of Confederates trying to drown the Pacific Railroad agent in the Osage River.
May 24, 1861	Field Officer C. Glover wrote his commanding officer, Colonel Blair, about Jackson's Ruffians and the finding of kegs of gunpowder at Chamois and Castle Rock, Missouri. With stores of powder, the Confederates had the

capability to destroy Union equipment, bridges, and trains.

| June 12, 1861 | From the Missouri Democrat, it was learned that the Gasconade and Osage Bridge had been destroyed. For this, the Rolla Fourteen received interrogation. |

June 12, 1861 From the Missouri Democrat, it was learned that the Gasconade and Osage Bridge had been destroyed. For this, the Rolla Fourteen received interrogation.

June 14, 1861 In this part of the report, the speakers (Union troops) are discussing how those supporting Governor Jackson and the rebels should be regarded as traitors. In as much, the report revealed a growing animosity toward Missouri farmers.

March 9, 1862 Union Post Rolla Report: During operations, it was reported that two men of the 1st Missouri Cavalry had been murdered by Rebels while on home leave. It was also reported that at Camp Coleman, there were bands of between 6 and 20 Confederates robbing and plundering.

June 5, 1862 Official date when the fourteen citizens in Rolla were first arrested by the Provost. Wesley Riden showed up among the prisoners.

August 16, 1862 Date of Wesley Riden's second arrest by the Provost.

September 4, 1862 Union report stated: "The whole Missouri country was full of bushwhackers."

September 5, 1862 to April 1864
The Union Army retracted and returned to concentrate on the eastern battlefield where the Union was on the ropes of defeat. Reports

went silent until May 1864. Wesley Riden had been killed two months before the reports started up again.

From various officer accounts, Union commanders amalgamated Confederate troops and bushwhackers together. I had not been convinced that they actually understood how to differentiate between them. Wesley Riden and the children had been killed nine months after the bombing of the Gasconade and Osage bridges. It was no mistake to believe that after the bombings, Union forces wanted revenge.

Eventually replaced by Grant, General Henry Halleck's order to kill guerillas did as much to doom Wesley Riden as any person or combat unit. In his pursuit of bridge burners, Halleck issued instructions directing federal soldiers to "immediately shoot" saboteurs caught in the act and military commissions to "execute" those tried and found guilty (Erwin, 2013). The eyewitness accounts, however, never stipulated that they had seen Wesley Riden commit a hostile act or set fire to property prior to his death. Clearly, the Halleck order opened the door to "friendly fire" on Missouri farmers.

After the second arrest, Wesley's case never went to trial. Riden had been killed walking down a road. General Halleck's order motivated Union soldiers to shoot first and ask questions later. In a letter he wrote to Senator Thomas Ewing Sr., one discovered the evils that men do:

> Our army here is almost as much in a hostile country as it was when in Mexico…It must be done; there is no other remedy. If I am sustained by the government, well and good; if not, I will take the consequences (Erwin, 2013, p. 30).

Clearly, Halleck and George Armstrong Custer belonged in the same company. In the Mexican-American War of course, our country fought an enemy, not other Americans. In a certain manner, Halleck acted with insubordination because he thought himself beyond the constraints of law. Halleck's hate speech proved to be indicative of how American Indians would later be regarded in the 1870s.

Union commanders abused their privileges as gentleman. Archived county reports highlighted the following towns where Confederates had been spotted and problems had been reported by unit leaders to their superiors:

> Osage and the Osage River located 73 miles from Big Piney where the Riden's were killed; Chamois located east of Jefferson City on the road to St. Louis; Castle Rock located to the southwest of Jefferson City; St. Aubert's and Fulton located northeast of Jefferson City; and Lanes Prairie located in the south a short distance of eighteen miles from Rolla (Osage County.org & Cornell University Library-USWD, 2015).

By May 14, 1864 two months after the Riden deaths, Union accounts said that twenty Rebels had been spotted at Vienna, Missouri (Osage County.org & Cornell University Library-USWD, 2015) located twenty-five miles from the Union command at Rolla. Big Piney was forty-two miles from Rolla, a brief travel for a Union cavalry unit carrying cannon.

According to the *Provost Marshall Papers*, Wesley Riden had been one of thirteen others arrested on June 5, 1862 for conspiracy to commit guerilla warfare by plotting to blow up a train. The Provost's Office regarded the detained as Rebels, and yet Wesley Riden's name never appeared on Erwin's (2012) list of guerillas.

Once arrested, men had the opportunity to shift their alliance by joining the Union Army or enrolling in the Missouri Militia. In muster roll records, l discovered a multiplicity of identical names being displayed. Employing multifarious sources from state records such as

Missouri Digital Heritage, I assigned case numbers to the Rolla Fourteen with specificity on the prisoners name, military unit, muster roll card, and how they had died if applicable (See Appendix C).

The current analysis showed that one captain and possibly one junior officer and one junior non-commissioned officer had been originally arrested in June 1862. Of the Rolla Fourteen, Wesley Riden's military file was never found. Certainly, records had confirmed his service in the MSG. After speaking with the Court Clerk of Texas County, a fire may have destroyed facts about his military experience. Apparently, arson was a common event during the Civil War. It seemed important to remember that records were being sought on a man born of an original pioneer family who arrived in Missouri 198 years ago.

Furthermore, I was unsuccessful at locating an officers commission of record. Wesley's arrest failed to stipulate an officer rank. Thus, doubt crept into the research in that the rank of captain may not have been Wesley Riden's official title. But if that were true, then his loss of life would have been murder, not a military kill. Thus, a civilian had been slain by the government. Following such logic would have therefore meant that Riden, a civilian, was simply utilizing his rights of free speech. Halleck had mastered the job of suspending these civil liberties.

A person's First Amendment rights were null and void in a world pressed by the loyalties of war. Allegiance oaths were offered to Confederates taken prisoner. In 1863, the president announced his *Ten-Percent Plan of Reconstruction* which stated "that amnesty and the full restoration of rights would be granted to all white southerners who took an oath affirming loyalty to the Union and support for emancipation" (Foner, 2006, p. 470). When allegiance oaths were refused, men were hunted down and slaughtered by federal agents, Union cavalry, and infantry units.

I considered the eyewitness' point about the demand for money. The truth was that both sides committed horrific atrocities and did so for monetary reward. Enter the record of Alf Bowlin, with archived statements made by Union soldier Sergeant Wellington Allen:

Lowry City, MO. Dec 28th 1885. I was Second Sergeant of Company B 1st Cavalry Regt. In December 1862, I was acting Orderly Sergeant of said company and my command reached Forsyth [Missouri] some time about the last of said month. We remained there till sometime in April 1863. While stationed at Forsyth, one Zack Thomas of Co A [of] my Regt. and one Nelson a confederate soldier who was then a paroled prisoner came to Forsyth from Springfield [and] they stayed with me in my tent the night they arrived at Forsyth. They told me that they were going to capture Alf Bowlin for whom a reward of $5,000.00 had been offered by the then acting governor of Mo., the said Bowlin to be captured alive or dead or his head to be presented for identification at Jefferson City. Thomas and Nelson left my tent in the morning the next day after they arrived and went to Nelson's House which was a double log cabin situated near the site of the Layton's Steam Saw Mill which was situated some 13 or 14 miles south of Forsyth and had been previously burned by the 2nd Mo. Cav. Along in the evening of the next day after Thomas and Nelson left my tent, Thomas returned alone and reported that he had killed Alf Bowlin (State Historical Society of Missouri Civil War Manuscripts, Western Historical Manuscript Collection, 1885).

Maj. McDermit of the 1st Iowa Cav. made a detail of 25 or 30 men as an escort and two six-mule teams and wagons who went with Thomas to where Nelson lived and brought in Alf Bowlin's body and Nelson's family and household goods arriving in Forsyth sometime in the night. The next morning

Bowlin's head was severed from his body and the body was burned somewhere in the vicinity of Forsyth. I did not see it burned but I saw Bowlin lying in the wagon before his head was severed from his body. I was detailed and had charge of the detachment with teams that took Bowlin's head together with Nelson and his family and household goods to Ozark Christian County Mo. at which point we arrived in the afternoon. A number of the citizens of Ozark and vicinity [were] having doubts as to whether it was really Alf Bowlin's head. [We] had the box containing the head. [It] was then opened for the first time and was identified by a number [of citizens] as being Bowlin's head. [We] then enclosed the head again in the box and proceeded on to Springfield (State Historical Society of Missouri Civil War Manuscripts, Western Historical Manuscript Collection, 1885).

Sergeant Allen and Bravo Company were in Forsyth, Missouri in 1863, a year before the Riden's were killed. Clearly from the evidence, if the Union was going to cut a man's head off, blowing them away with cannon did not seem such an unlikely event or method.

Commensurate with Wesley Riden, I was unable to locate a military record on Alf Bowlin as well as derivatives of his name such as Alfred Bowling. Reading more of the statements of Allen, on the very last page could be found the discovery that Alf Bowlin could have been named Alf Bolen (State Historical Society of Missouri Civil War Manuscripts, Western Historical Manuscript Collection, 1885). Another check found no military record or grave site with the name however. I had not expected to find a burial of Alf since his body had been mutilated.

All the wading through the mud of research paid off when I was able to clarify that the Alf Bowlin I had been looking for all this time had been the famous bushwhacker, Alf Bolin. Apparently, Bolin's antics caused him to be wanted by the Union, dead or alive. Expiry seemed preferable. I considered the possibility that Alf Bolin may have been involved in the Riden killings.

According to the Taney Project (2015), Bolin and his gang of roughly 20 men had been considered ruthless, fearsome renegades during the Civil War and were known to be the cause of orchestrated ambushes on citizens and the Union Army in Southwest Missouri and Northwest Arkansas. As evidence, researchers were able to tie in Bolin's part in a homicide: Bolin's gang killed two Union soldiers returning to the army after a furlough home. The soldiers had been slain near "Murder Rocks" and buried by Joe McGill on what was now known as the Charley Mahnkey Place (Taney Project, 2015).

It appeared that conspirators and Confederate soldiers who were hunted down and slain were not showing up in the war manuscripts. In some of the records, Alf Bolin was said to be a Confederate soldier, but this could not be corroborated. So far, the same held true for Wesley Riden. On the other hand, what began to take shape was verification that both Bolin and Wesley Riden owned property. I could not pass over the fact that people knew where the Riden's lived.

The Union, in as much, would have had access to who the landowners were in the county records. As seen in the statements by Wellington Allen, the Union utilized intelligence gathering from former prisoners to target who they considered conspirators. Someone told on Wesley Riden for speaking publicly against the Union.

For every John F. Kennedy, there was a Lee Harvey Oswald. For every Chief Black Kettle, there posited a George Armstrong Custer. For every Dr. Martin Luther King, there remained a James Earl Ray. For every murder, there was an assassin to be assigned. With passion, I sought to know what unit had been involved in the Riden killings and what commander or sergeant gave the order to shoot. My blood-hound ways had picked up a trail in the Missouri and Western Heritage Collections.

The information on Bolin established two points germane to law: First, unlike Bolin the bushwhacker, Wesley Riden had not been charged with the high crime of killing old men, women, or children when he was arrested in 1862. His first arrest had been based on an unsubstantiated claim of espionage in which the government would have had to prove motive and intent. His second arrest centered on the freedom to speak in a public arena, where of course by 1864, had been up for grabs.

Second, like the Bolin case, Wesley Riden had been sought out and killed in an extremely violent manner. The cases were opposable but yet had resulted in eerily similar conclusions. Wesley Riden had been exterminated for what he might have said rather than for what he might have done. Archived evidence pointed out that Bolin, on the other hand, had slew seven members of the 6th Missouri Round Pond Convalescents (State Historical Society of Missouri Civil War Manuscripts, Western Historical Manuscript Collection, 1885).

The location of Wesley Riden's two arrests, Rolla and Waynesville, had been centrally associated with Union and Confederate commander's reports coming in from the field. Rolla sat northeast of Waynesville approximately twenty-eight miles. The following list of synthesized qualitative data from Missouri Digital Heritage (2007, 1889) appeared relevant:

Dec. 1861   Ground combat began between regular army troops and militias loyal to the Union and Confederate soldiers and guerillas loyal to the South. Including Carthage, the first major actions occurred in the grid formed by the Big and Little Piney Rivers, Licking, Hartville, Waynesville, and Houston townships. [Riden lived near the Big Piney River]

Jun. 1862   Colonel A. Sigel with the 5th Missouri State Militia (MSM) Cavalry occupied Waynesville. Sigel was in charge of four companies serving to protect Wright, Webster, and Texas County. Sigel's units had daily encounters with Confederate recruiting parties, guerillas, and bushwhackers. Skirmishing had occurred near Licking, Missouri. Confederate guerillas were killed, wounded, and dispersed (Digital County Records, p. 454). [Licking is a place that holds Riden burials]

Jun. 5, 1862   Date of Wesley Riden's first arrest (Provost Records).

Jun. 7, 1862   Sigel captured the Confederate camp and equipment at Little Piney River. [Wesley Riden was in jail at this time]

Aug. 1862   Month of Wesley Riden's second arrest (Provost Records)

Nov. 26, 62   General F.H. Warren's Report at Hartville, Missouri: Hartville and Houston, Missouri were strongholds of Union militia. Warren reported that he could not follow the Confederates but that they "were all after trains" (Digital County Records, p. 454-455). [Riden's accusation]

Jan. 1863   Confederate Major General Marmaduke's expedition arrived in Missouri and participated in the Battle of Hartville, Wright County. [Riden's established first school in Hartville and served in first local government]

Sept. 1863   From Houston, Captain Richard Murphy (Union) started dispatching scouts and small teams to capture or kill guerillas and to bring back captured soldiers

(Digital County Records, p. 456). [Riden's disposition]

Nov. 1863   Corporal Calvin Blankenship KIA. He was considered a bushwhacker (Digital County Records, p. 456). Union and Confederate soldiers moved into winter camps. After December, 1863, Texas County History Records ended temporarily in the archives.

Mar. 1, 64   Date when Wesley Riden and child or children were slain near Big Piney River. Big Piney had been located on a stretch of distance between Waynesville and Houston. Big Piney was 42 miles southwest from Rolla.

Nov. 1864   History record picks back up date-wise. Foxtrot Company of the 5th MSM Cavalry had been posted at Little Piney River (Digital County Records, p. 456).

Thus far, I could tell from this and previous information that important clues were beginning to align: The Riden's held roots in the Hartville School System. Wesley Riden had been a businessman with his father Joseph Sr. during the 1840s and 1850s in Hartville. The father and sons owned property in the area. At present, the military evidence pointed to the 5th MSM Cavalry being in the area before and after the Riden murders. I also noted that eight months of records had vanished.

The killing of Confederate Corporal Calvin Blankenship appeared relevant because the Riden's and Blankenship's had been joined by marriage. Also killed in 1864, Calvin had been buried in the Mitchell Cemetery at Licking. The Foxtrot Company Commander who had been in the Piney River region in 1864 may have been Captain John B. Van Sant. The following Union officers became characters of interest: General F. H. Warren, Colonel A. Sigel, Captain Richard Murphy, and Captain Van Sant.

General F. H. Warren Initially, General Warren fought in Missouri. He received orders from the U.S. War Department to report to Chambersburg, Pa. in July 1863 (Civil War Index-Gettysburg, p. 728).

Colonel A. Sigel Confirmed by Civil War Officer Index – Missouri to be at his rank and had served in the 5th MSM.

Captain R. Murphy Confirmed by Civil War Index –Little Rock, Arkansas to be assigned to the 5th MSM Cavalry at Houston and organized under the District Command at Rolla. Murphy commanded two companies, Bravo and Golf Company.

Captain J.B. Van Sant Letter to his superior officer from Independence, Mo command confirmed that Captain Van Sant commanded Company F in November - December 1862. His duty at the time had been to help escort Kansas volunteers to the state line (U. California Library, 1890, p. 824, 846).

To have argued that one of these officers performed the actual killings had not been my intention. I did project however that one of their junior officers or NCOs (Non-commissioned Officers) may have stumbled upon the Riden farm. General Warren would not have knowledge of the Riden deaths because he received orders to Pennsylvania in 1863. One very important aspect appeared true: Given the duplicity of battles taking place in Missouri and the counties in which they had occurred, Wesley and his family would have been surrounded by combatants, especially soldiers attached to the Fifth Missouri. The antithetical firecracker looked to be connected to the command of Colonel Sigel who had spent three years serving in the area the Riden family members frequented. Captain Murphy would have heard of Wesley Riden in Rolla.

The Rolla District had been the first agency to arrest Wesley Riden so when he was arrested a second time in Waynesville, the Federals already had paperwork on him. By name, the officers who had made both seizures were unknown to me at present. Loyal to Union malfeasance, Missouri volunteer and militia units began fiercely tracking-down Confederates, guerillas and bushwhackers throughout south-central Missouri, and especially within the Piney area where commanders of the 5th MSM had concentrated their efforts.

Sometimes numbering more than twenty-strong, MSM riders accepted reconnaissance missions deep into the Missouri jungles. Operations ran continually. Contact was authorized. Cavalry teams of men had the authority of judges to take a person's life at any time, on the spot, right in front of God, his wife, and his children. Union commanders granted no quarter.

The 5th MSM Regiment had two service periods in the indexes. According to Dyer (1908, p. 1306), the first time the regiment organized had been at St. Joseph, Missouri in March, 1862 and became attached to the District of Central Missouri. This regiment served operations in Carroll, Ray and Livingston Counties on July 27 to August 4, at Grand River on August 1, near Barry Section on August 14, in Iron County on September 11, at Liberty and Sibley's Landing on October 6, at the California House on October 18, and then in Independence on February 3, 1863 (Dyer, p. 1306). It was not my belief that the "Old 5th" Regiment interacted in any way with the troubles near Licking and Big Piney. Come to find out, this first regiment had been hit hard by disease (Dyer, p. 1306) forcing it to be reorganized.

The reshaped 5th MSM Regiment experienced more combat scenes than its original muster. Ordered into action on February 2,

1863 from a synthesized regrouping of the 13th Regiment MSM Cavalry, the 5th Regiment accepted duty at the District of Rolla and served at this location through July 8, 1865 (Dyer, 1908, p. 1306). Wesley Riden had already been arrested twice when the 5th reorganized and reactivated. Its appearance and return to battle showed clearly to be within in the timeframe of the Riden deaths.

As compiled by Dyer (1908), the 1863-1864 combat record of the newly arranged 5th MSM Regiment was extensive, which I condensed for clarity:

Feb. 8, 1863   Service at Independence, Mo. with Charlie, Delta and Foxtrot Company in place. The 5th maintained a headquarters at Waynesville.

Jun. 20, 1863   Scouts from Hotel Company were sent out for a three-day mission.

July 3, 1863   Delta Company skirmished with enemy forces.

Aug. 6-11, 63   Scouting from Houston to Spring River Mills and skirmished with the enemy. Company Bravo, Charlie, Foxtrot, and Golf became engaged.

Aug. to Oct., 63 Detachments were sent to Jack's Ford, Warrensville, Texas County, near Houston, near Salem with Charlie and Mike Company, near Man's Creek, at King's House, and near Waynesville with Hotel Company.

Nov. & Dec. 1863 Scouting from Houston to Jack's Fork with Bravo, Golf, and India Company. Scouting from Salem with Charlie and Mike Company.

Feb. 5-17, 1864 Scouts sent from Houston into Arkansas and skirmished with the enemy. July 5-6, 1864 Scout team reconnoitered Big Piney.

July to July, 64-65 Scouting teams continued to be sent into the area until the 5th Regiment mustered out.

Scouts served as recon units on horseback. In all, eight companies had been utilized by the 5th MSM according to Dyer's work. The mission into Arkansas in February 1864 raised an eyebrow in that once the assignment had been completed, the teams may have filtered back individually to their posts at Houston. This line of logic offered some remarkable level of corroboration with eyewitness statements that a Union squad came upon Riden suddenly and by happenstance. But if the scouts came from a base in Houston, they would have never reached as far North as Big Piney. At least not under military orders. While it was true that a scout team reconnoitered Big Piney, that mission occurred in July 1864 about four months after the Riden deaths. More and more, I became convinced that select members of the 5th MSM had killed my great uncle and at least one cousin.

Essentially, Wesley Riden had been surrounded. Union scouts were positioned at bases in the South like Houston. The Union had a well-fortified installation at Rolla. I found that Dyer (1908) offered no casualty numbers or Confederates or guerillas by name. Therefore, while the geographic points cleared the way for establishing what units may have been in the area of Wesley Riden's dwelling, and moreover that soldiers serving in the 5th MSM had much ado with the situation, I could not hang the murders on any one person or commander.

In fairness, Dyer's (1908) work offered good insight because he had been able to differentiate the service periods and locations of service between the two regiments: The first organization of the 5th MSM Regiment had not served in any of the Missouri counties where Wesley Riden had lived. Nothing insinuated that companies of the original 5th had ever gone into the Rolla or Waynesville area where Wesley Riden had been arrested in 1862. The nugget from Dyer's work appeared in the 1863-1864 scouting reports of the second 5th MSM.

Documented reports indicated that after the undertaking into Arkansas, the 5th MSM never sent out any more scout teams until the middle of summer. Consequentially, it seemed proper to have asked: What was the 5th MSM Regiment doing from February 18 through July 4? After all, the regiment was a militia unit, not a regular army outfit. Had the soldiers of the regiment been placed on extended liberty or released? Were soldiers from the regiment roaming the countryside aimlessly? I believed that they were, which supports eyewitness accounts of the murders.

I envisioned Great Uncle Wesley Riden to be a man of few fears. Obviously, he felt comfortable taking a walk with one of the twins in an area that had become wrought with guerillas and bushwhackers. I supposed that Wesley garnered his confidence from being a local community leader. His family tree had farmed Missouri in the years before the great migration westward. On the same day that Wesley died, Ulysses S. Grant received a promotion to general.

Wesley Riden had a family to feed, a field to plow, and a platoon of dragoons relying on his leadership should the need arise. One of the definitive points that had been made in the literature appeared to be the fact that citizens like Riden found themselves in winless situations during the war. In finality, the acceptable argument seemed to be that the murders occurred by chance. And yet several questions remained: Why did the soldiers think Wesley had money? What kind of monsters would kill a baby? Who would shoot an old man?

In Missouri, the Federals frequently used state militias against its own citizenry forcing Missourians to do things against their will. Elizabeth Thompson was forced to sell products in her general store only to Union troops (Daniels Letter, 1862). Distrust prevailed socially. People turned on one another. Evidently, four citizens filed affidavits with the Union Provost against Moniteau farmer Coleman

Bruce for "vocalizing with distain" his displeasure with the U.S. government (Community & Conflict, No. 3437). Thompson and Bruce remained alive, but Wesley Riden lay dead.

People believed cannon had been used to take down Riden and his infant. Less attention had been paid to horse artillery brigades which had been staffed with regular army personnel, not militiamen according to Morgan (1990). The distinction seemed highly relevant. I found it difficult to believe that a wandering militia unit, pretending for a second that it had been men from the 5th MSM, would have had the authority to carry an artillery piece. I supported Morgan's inclination that the soldiers who killed the Riden's were active duty personnel.

Located midway between St. Louis and Springfield, Rolla became the county seat of Phelps County four years before the Civil War. Militarily, Rolla held the gate key for entrance into Southwest Missouri. The Rolla District held original jurisdiction on Riden legally. Once serving as the tribal mainstay of Shawnee Indians, the following Union officers were believed to have commanded units made up of men from Rolla, Phelps County:

> Phelps County residents took part in several military regiments. These included the 32nd Missouri Volunteers under Lieutenant Colonel Warmoth; the 7th Missouri Cavalry under Colonel Bowen; the Rolla Guards under Captain Tiffany; the Phelps County Militia under Major C.P. Walker; and the 9th Missouri Cavalry (Goodspeed, 1971).

Lieutenant Colonel Henry C. Warmoth had indeed led the 32nd Missouri Volunteers during the Civil War. Three years following service, Colonel Warmoth became one of Louisiana's youngest governors. A man of integrity and gentlemanly occupation, I did not believe he had something to do with the Ridens' demise. Warmouth himself died in 1931 and could be found buried with honor at Orleans

Parrish, Louisiana. Captain Ezra Tiffany had commanded Golf Company in the 63rd Regiment Enrolled Missouri Militia (EMM). Information on Major Charles P. Walker of the Phelps County Militia had not been identified.

In a hunt for information on the 7th Missouri Cavalry and the officer named Bowen, records were discovered from Goodspeed (1888) on a Lieutenant Colonel William D. Bowen which revealed that he had slain a senior Union officer, Colonel F.M. Cornyn, in 1863. Bowen and Cornyn had been assigned to the newly formed 10th Missouri Cavalry Volunteers who were partials of Bowen's Battalion of Volunteers, the 7th Cavalry, and the 9th Missouri Cavalry Volunteers (Goodspeed, 1888, p. 254). Apparently Bowen enjoyed killing officers. Did he kill Captain Wesley Riden? The possibility existed, however it seemed worth noting that unlike Uncle Fil who knew General Lyon was an officer, none of the eyewitnesses remembered seeing someone with silver on their shoulders.

On March 23, 2018, I toured and analyzed the battlefields at Pea Ridge National Military Park. In the Battle of Elk Horn Tavern, Bowen's Cavalry carried the M1841 Mountain Howitzer employed by the U.S. Army for use in rugged terrain. Introduced during the Mexican-American War, this kind of howitzer could be pulled by a single horse or carried on the backs of three horses. Given the area and timeframe, along with the portability of the weapon itself, I believed whole-heartedly that, based on secondary evidence, the M1841 had been used to kill the Riden's. I could not pin it on Colonel Bowen at the moment.

Most of the commissioned officers who fought in Missouri and Arkansas rostered as outsiders. Captain Wesley Riden could have been slain by outsiders who did not know he was a prominent farmer or justice's son. It could not have been a local militia. They would have been familiar with the location of his farm. The eyewitnesses would have been able to identify the culprits by name. Being killed by a gang of strangers to the area did support the theory that the deaths occurred by happenstance. Again, I think the men were serving on active duty.

Two native Germans, Osterhaus and Sigel, were among the Union officers staff that battled at Pea Ridge. With the exception of Stand Watie's new residence, all of the generals who commanded troops at Pea Ridge came from other regions of the United States: Earl Van Dorn, Mississippi; Sterling Price, Virginia; Benjamin McCulloch, Tennessee; Albert Pike, Massachusetts; Samuel Curtis, New York; Franz Sigel, Baden, Germany; Peter Osterhaus, Koblenz, Germany; Grenville Dodge, Massachusetts; and Jefferson C. Davis, Indiana.

With respect to strangers, during my searching, the infamous James Butler Hickok (1837-1876) turned up. While casting a line into the Rolla Archives, Hickok appeared in a collection of papers written by Missourians stressed by the charades of rebellion. Although argumentative and even bombastic in the eyes of some, I held no uncertainty that based on where Hickok had traveled in and out of Southwest Missouri from 1861 to 1865, the probability that he and Captain Wesley Riden's path had crossed proved strong. Did I believe that Hickok wanted Riden dead? I did not, however I believed he knew of the killings. I could not envision   Hickok strapping himself with cannon.

Born in Illinois, Hickok came to Kansas and Missouri with the Civil War, a young man at 24 years old. Sources about Hickok's exploits covered the popular things about his life like his time in Deadwood, South Dakota or Abilene, Texas. Such unfortunate oversight missed the essence of his lawful beginning. While historians had stocked book shelves with rhetoric about who killed Wild Bill Hickok, it was actually Missouri and the war that made him legendary. Others might have argued that Bill's gunfight against Dave Tutt in

Springfield in 1865 gave him tremendous notoriety. During the war, Hickok sided with the Union and in fact became a Jayhawker.

Not even Hickok or the long arm of the law could hold back the wave of vengefulness that Missourians shared for their Union conquerors. In his twenties, Hickok became an enforcer of the law. He wanted to make a name for himself and he did just that. Hickok figured out that the frontier would be the perfect medium to develop his skills. I felt firm in stating that Hickok may have caught wind about the plot to blow up the Gasconade Train. It would have been something an eager beaver like Hickok would jump on.

People talked. Word spread fast in country communities like Duke and Big Piney. According to *Community and Conflict*, Hickok earned his unique nickname "from his actions against Confederate guerillas" (para. 1, No. 585). History showed that Hickok had worked for the Union Provost's Office. Speculative evidence based on Hickok's movements revealed that an informal meeting between Hickok and Captain Riden could have occurred while Hickok was serving in Springfield and Rolla (Community & Conflict, No. 585). The stated facts:

April 1861   Civil War erupted between the states. Hickok became a scout and spy for the Union (para. 1).

Fall 1861   Hickok signed on as a teamster with the Union Army at Sedalia, Mo. and became assigned to Springfield and Rolla (para. 4).

Dec. 31, 1861 At the end of the year, Hickok was serving as a wagon master (para. 4).

Sept. 1862   For an undisclosed reason, he leaves his trade and disappears. Historians believed that this was the period when Hickok started   spying for the Federals (para. 5).

Sept. 1863   Hickok reappeared as a police detective employed by the S.W. Missouri Provost Marshall. His duties included monitoring soldiers who frequented Springfield saloons while on duty and checking ownership of liquor licenses. Hickok often made trips to Little Rock, Arkansas where he arrested men and collected Union debts (para. 5, 6).

After 1863   Hickok signed up as a scout under the command of General Sanborn at Rolla District (para. 6).

June 1865   Hickok mustered out as a scout (para. 7).

I believed that Hickok had been briefed on the antics of Captain Riden while serving under Sanborn. Wild Bill tried to play James Bond in a Wild West Missouri where men could not be trusted. As the evidence showed, Hickok spied on Springfield soldiers. The following information appeared in files from the *Union Provost Marshal's Papers* relevant to the death timeline of Captain Wesley Riden:

Oct. 21, 1863   Mr. Isaac Warmoth filed a complaint to a Colonel Broadhead about an old man being shot and killed trying to stop robbers on his property.

Mar. 1-15, 1864   Captain Riden and children were killed but not listed in the Provost's file anywhere as being deceased.

April 22, 1864   The Provost compiled a list of 71 influential Phelps County residents and their political status.

May 9, 1864   Mr. Peck provided a deposition to the Provost
                     about "Rebel sympathizers" and "parties guilty
                     of swaying command."

June 10, 1864   Report from the Provost that John York had
                     been murdered in February 1864.

The complaint filed in the fall of 1863 by Isaac Warmouth resembled the Riden death scene with one major difference: eyewitnesses in the Riden cases identified the offenders as Union cavalry pulling cannon. Robbery seemed to be the commonality. Provost records did not mention the Riden deaths however which I found odd. Peck's entry in May proved even one's neighbor could not be reliable. Farm land had been trampled by Union soldiers, thus Missouri farmers had a right to be angry. Nothing had been discussed about Peck turning in Riden specifically but the circumstance existed in theory. York's murder occurred one month before Riden's. The idea of swaying command may at first appear to fit Riden but the things he said had been made to an audience of civilians.

Warmouth himself had an interesting story to tell. At one time, he had broken the law and been placed on parole for giving out blank property permits. The Union actually questioned which side of the war he favored because his name had appeared in documents auspicious to the Rebel cause. Unlike Riden, Mr. Warmouth had never been killed for his misgivings. The April 22 entry seemed convincing: The Union Provost appeared to be looking for more political prisoners. Within two months following the Ridens' expiry, the Provost appeared to be excessively concerned about citizen-driven political involvement.

Summarily, I embraced final thoughts on the Riden murders: Wesley Riden would have been known by northern commanders and local authorities in Rolla or Waynesville. Because the family had extensive pioneer roots in Texas County, Wesley would not have been a stranger to southern jurisdictions. He and his brother, and perhaps even their father, had served in theMissouri State Guard before the Civil War began. To be clear, however, I could not completely feel satisfied that he had served officially in a military capacity. Following two arrests, Wesley had never been sent to a Union prison. If Riden held to be a civilian, then 'murder' would be the correct designator by the law.

Unlike his brother's grave which had been decorated with an American flag clearly revealing that he had been honored as a veteran, Wesley's remains were never truly discoverable. Furthermore, the State of Missouri had failed to list him as a soldier in the archives. Even though the oldest Texas County records building had been burned, I expected the state to hold a military file on Wesley Riden which it did not. Nothing had been written if he had fought at Pea Ridge, so close to home.

Historically, Pea Ridge had been a major engagement and victory for the Union that would allow it to secure Missouri as a state in the hands of the Federals. If the Union would have lost at Pea Ridge, the Confederates would have regained control in central and southwest Missouri. The Union had previously been defeated at Wilson's Creek in 1861. After winning at Pea Ridge, fragmented Union cavalry units remained in areas like Big Piney. The outfits were active duty members, not militia, which matched the facts in the case as told by the eye-witnesses describing the appearance of the group. An unsolved nagging question remained: Was an active duty unit sent under orders to find Wesley Riden and kill him?

Colonel Bowen's unit had carried the howitzer which I believed had been the murder weapon. The howitzer could handle being pulled over the rocky terrain in the area around Riden's farm. If not from Bowen's outfit, it would have been used by other complementary units of the Union that had remained after the Pea

Ridge conflict. Colonel Sigel's unit could also be suspected. Bowen had a private in his battalion serving under the name John Reariden.

I had decided that I could not give Hickok a pass on the murders. He had paperwork on Riden's arrests. Furthermore, he had been marked as a spy for the Union based out of Rolla. Hickok had been going back and forth to Springfield gathering intelligence. He knew the Big Piney area and that the Riden's had a cave. Obviously, someone told him that Riden had been speaking out against the Union with 13 others. Why else would the Provost's Office start compiling political registers one month after his death? Moreover, how could a military record simply just disappear? It seemed to be a matter of picking between horseshoes and hand grenades.

CHAPTER FOUR

Horseshoes and Hand Grenades

Happenstance I doubted. Murder seemed more likely. My impression: Federals wanted my great uncle dead so they killed him for trying to 'sway command.' The evidence displayed motive and intent. No matter how grotesque, men followed orders. When the mission came down to rub out Captain Wesley Riden, his conspirators acted decisively. But what price would one man's life be worth in the trading of millions of souls? "Let us start talking falsely now, the hour's getting late" (Bob Dylan, *All Along the Watchtower*, 1967).

Horseshoes: Military and non-military families caught up in the chaos of combat suffered tremendously during the Civil War, especially children and the elderly. Those unique first-travelers who ventured or had been forcefully removed onto the Great Plains modeled brave Americans whom exuded a willingness to survive, adapt, and endure. Pioneer farmers and the Five Tribes embodied the concepts of true grit, hard work, and religious faith. But that was before the World exploded.

Hand grenades: I shuddered at the thought that nothing was left of Wesley Riden but a greasy spot. Sadly, his story and that of my cousins played out time and time again during the Civil War. The killings had not been the first time I felt the personal sting of death (See *Bloodied Dress Blues*). Although one might have argued that Riden died as a combatant during a time of extreme conflict, that same assertion could not be stated so cleverly with respect to the twin infants who died. For now, I became satisfied that their story had finally found print.

As I watched and learned, a core ingredient of my inheritance appeared: North Carolinian Great Grandmother Susanna Riden held two different gene surnames: *Gynosgisy Soquilli* and *Sukwi Soquilli*. I found her to be the mother of Joseph Warren Riden Sr. and married to James Riden III who went by the nickname, Jesse. A fifth-generation Native American ancestor, Susanna's surnames reflected descent from the Eastern Band of the Cherokee Nation.

In my dreams, I watched Susanna find life near Bryson City, North Carolina where the Great Creator gave the laws and fire to the Cherokee. Oddly, when I looked at the distance from Bryson City to the Pendleton District in South Carolina where Leonard Garrett situated his farm, it was less than one-hundred miles. I waited to confirm Susanna's birth and death dates because the age of her husband Jesse appeared noticeably older. For the times however, this fact did not appear uncommon: the fur trapper had claimed a trophy wife.

Information regarding James "Jesse" Riden's biographical detail had been mentioned in scuttlebutt from a *Riden Message Board* about his occupation, his son and the Garrett family:

Joseph Riden b 1797 in Pendleton District, South Carolina, son of James Riden a fur trader. Joseph Riden married Elizabeth "Betsy" Garrett and she was born 1792 in Pittsylvania County, VA; daughter of Leonard Garrett & Margaret Gover. I have a copy of Leonard Garrett Estate Papers to heirs, his children, Wesley, John, Nancy Dent, Henry Garrett & Elizabeth Riden and William Garrett as children of Leonard Garrett Feb 1, 1826 in St Francois County, MO. (Post by Michael E. Eberhart, 2011).

If Jesse Riden became a mountain man whose business involved fur trading, then his marriage to Susanna made cultural sense. The geography of the northwest corner of South Carolina favored freshwater trapping and an abundance of water resources for small farms.

The post by Eberhart appeared to be spot-on with respect to the Garrett nuclear family. It became the first time I had heard of Elizabeth being referred to as "Betsy." A brilliant Arkansas statesman in his own right, her brother Wesley and her husband Joseph Riden Sr. became extraordinary men in their small communities. I expected the DNA analysis to reflect more insight, but it failed to do so.

The code of my becoming a human began in the Pendleton District in South Carolina by way of a crucial decision that Leonard Garrett made after fighting in the glorious American Revolution. Established as both a county and district in the 1800s, the Pendleton area had been where Leonard Garrett's daughter Elizabeth married Jesse Riden's son Joseph Sr. in 1817. As a reminder, Pendleton land had at one time been propertied by the Church of England but preceded in ownership by the Cherokee Nation for which Susannah would have belonged.

Joseph Sr. had been born in South Carolina thus making him a resident of the area when Leonard Garrett's family emigrated to Northwest South Carolina from Maryland, a trip greater than seven-hundred miles. My impression became that the Garrett's utilized the Great Wagon Road which passed through North Carolina, Susannah's birth state. When Leonard Garrett had been a private in the 3rd Maryland, he may have befriended Native Americans. We already know that fur trappers became trading partners with many tribes.

Exhausting a map featured in Powell (2006) coupled with Google Maps technology, I charted the passage the Garrett's would have taken from Maryland: Ten years after Valley Forge, Leonard had moved the family to Pittsylvania, Virginia where Elizabeth and all but one of her siblings were birthed. Her youngest brother William Thomas Garrett looked to be the only child born in Knox, Tennessee, 1794. Momentarily holding in place for William's birth, by the year 1810, Leonard had secured property in Greenville County, South Carolina where Elizabeth and Joseph Riden Sr. eventually hitched. The Riden's and Garrett's remained in South

Carolina during the War of 1812 but had relocated to Missouri by 1820.

Texas County historical records had shown previously that Joseph Riden Sr. became hugely successful in Missouri. Shortly after Elizabeth's death in 1852, he married Nancy Barry Truesdale. One puzzle remained: What push or pull factor sent the Garrett's and Riden's into Missouri? Why had the two families not stayed in South Carolina? In order to conclude this book, I needed to know these answers. Moreover, the ghosts would not accept indecision on the matter.

Beforehand, I had considered three major themes that may have led to the decision to leave South Carolina: The Era of Manifest Destiny, the families avoidance of slavery, and the brothers' decisions to chase the timber or mining industry which had opened up by Missouri's acceptance into the Union. These years happened to be the pre-days of the Trail of Tears.

When Elizabeth married Joseph Sr. in 1817, her father had to be about 60 years old. Travel may have been difficult at his age. Why would not Leonard stay in South Carolina where he had invested in a sizable piece of property? If Joseph Sr. had Cherokee blood, the reason for leaving South Carolina could not have been Manifest Destiny because it was never an American concept until around 1845. Moreover, the families went to Missouri before gold had been discovered in Northern Georgia and they had traveled years before the presidency of Andrew Jackson. I wondered if the Garrett's and Joseph Sr. had sensed the political and social upheaval to come

Every time I tried to finish the book, the ghosts refused to give in to my intention. Pressing forward, I looked for intersecting knowledge between the Cherokee, the South Carolina Slave Narratives and the types of cultivation proceeding in the Pendleton District in the late 1700s. In some of the reading, I had noticed discussions on rice and malaria affecting slaves laboring in lowland plantation fields. Thus, the threat of disease may have forced

Leonard Garrett and his new son by marriage to rethink their residential decisions.

As a reminder of the record, the U.S. Census data indicated that Leonard Garrett had a young boy and his father who were documented as slaves that worked for him. Garrett did not own a plantation however. For a man living in South Carolina in this time period, that seemed rather unique. Ford Jr. (1988) showed that during the 1806 South Carolina Congressional Election, the Pendleton and Greenville Districts had the fewest slave populations in the state. Ford Jr. (1988) also revealed that the Eighth District had an extensive Baptist following.

Pendleton Baptists jockeyed for position on the slave question. Christians who went into the South after the American Revolution were probably the first religious people to express feelings of abolition. Grandmother Elizabeth had inherited Leonard's slaves which she gave freedom to twenty years before the Civil War. Clearly, she was against slavery. If her husband possessed a Cherokee bloodline, and the Eastern Nation practiced slavery which they did, the issue of enslaving humans would have cut deep in the Riden household.

At least in part, I felt comfortable with projecting that the Riden's left South Carolina because of many reasons including slavery. In fairness, I would remind the record that Garrett's two slaves did in fact accompany the Riden's into Missouri where they eventually gained their freedom. The South Carolina slave narratives never yielded a background or interviews with Garrett or Riden slaves in my family tree.

Treaties with the U.S. Government occurred around the same time frame that the Garrett's and Riden's pulled stakes and moved out of South Carolina. They landed in Missouri before the ink of the *Compromise* had dried. James Riden and Susanna Stolen Horse Riden headed for the mountains because of treaties and land acquisition. Obviously, both avoided Removal because they were never buried in Missouri. My great grandparents perished in North

Carolina somewhere in the *Sha-Kon-O-Hey*, land of the blue smoke also known to the white man as the Great Smoky Mountains. Eventually, they resurfaced in Pennsylvania.

Living in the Pendleton District, Leonard Garrett and his sons probably felt threatened of losing their farm by treaty. After all, his son-in-law had a Cherokee mother. By 1816, the Chickasaw, Cherokee, and Creek had seceded land to the government in treaties. By 1820, most of the Eastern lands had been carved up by the U.S. Government. The ways things continued to turn sour for Native Americans, my guess was that the decision to migrate may have been a collective decision.

Given the fact that Grandfather James Riden III employed in the fur trade, it seemed at least minimally possible that the Garrett's and Riden's started thinking about relocating to Missouri following the 1817 laws which prohibited Europeans from further trapping in United States Territory. St. Louis markets boomed with pelts in the early 1800s. I pondered over the possibility that John Jacob Astor's Northern Department of the American Fur Company had come up in family conversation. If the Garrett's and Riden's wanted to invest time in the fur trade however why not just stay in South Carolina where they had backdoor access to the uplands, plenty of water, and a bounty of available beaver?

Elizabeth's son Captain William Charles Riden had been born in St. Genevieve on the Mississippi River south of St. Louis. While fur looked rather appealing to the Garrett's and Riden's, patriarch Leonard Garrett became a farmer, not a trapper. One would have to work extremely hard in convincing me that Leonard would have taken such a risk. I even considered the possibility of a power struggle between Leonard and James. Eight years separated the two, both into middle age. The Garrett's and Riden's became farmers and cowboys, not fur trappers.

Then someone tossed a grenade into my bunker: From a private source, I discovered the fact that James III had served during the American Revolution when he was only twelve years old. Records showed his service began before the Garrett enlistments. Aligned with new evidence, I also came across information revealing that his father and my fifth-generation great grandfather John Riden had also served in Continental service. This was confirmed through the Fold3.com Revolutionary War Collection. Things moved into crazy: I found Riden-named soldiers serving on both sides in the War of 1812. At this point, I realized I would have to write a sequel to this book.

There were other themes of relevance with respect to migratory push factors that would have influenced the families to move westward: In the year 1814, Andrew Jackson had defeated the Creek Red Sticks at Horseshoe Bend. In 1817, he started the Seminole Wars. It seemed possible that the Garrett's and Riden's feared they might get caught up in a war against all Native Americans if Jackson's Army decided to turn West once Florida had capitulated. In 1819, the Adams-Onis Treaty reduced Spanish Territory and in turn opened the Missouri Territory giving the families a welcome opportunity.

Ghosts Be Silent

Although discomforting, conclusions were never finite. Journeys were never completely over. But now I had come to the end of the trail if not for temporary reasons. The bear and eagle had found sanctuary in my Ghost Dance. On the horizon, I saw the arrival of the great thundering herds of buffalo. In a sweet and low voice, I heard grandmother say, "come back to camp my little Elohi Awohali."

Riding a stolen horse, I had traveled a path of knowledge attainment while forced to accept truths about the ghosts in my life. Through the memories of ancestors, I discovered my own immortality. Who I claimed to be today had been distinctly relative to who I was in the past. This book was merely the beginning and not the end.

Affordable in this book, once hidden behind a door of obscurity, through oral tradition, the torch had been passed, the word transferred, the message sent. In this book, I tried to raise the dead. In doing so, I found ghosts of war sitting in fighting holes loading their weapons.

Time had of course been an enemy to us all. In finding the Old Baptist Cemetery at Birch Tree overgrown and in disarray, I experienced the truest of realities: human beings had returned to the dust from which they had been made. The curiosities that initially arose from the Oak Grove Graveyard turned into something bigger than anything I could have imagined. Toward the end of writing books, it had always amazed me that several hotel receipts, a million hand-written notes, and a billion thoughts originating from the central nervous system, could be condensed into a couple hundred pages of edited text.

The *Ghosts of War* encompassed real-life stories and situations as tangible as the changing of the seasons. I had no choice but to give the ghosts my devotion and time. I wanted to understand their struggles trying to survive a country in chaos. Thoreau once wrote "that the mass of men lead lives of quiet desperation" (Ruchti, 2016, Abstract). While that may have been indicative for riverboat captains, life on the frontier for the ghosts was anything but quiet and mundane.

Throughout this book, when I would uncover a ghost of war, more ghosts appeared. By now, one may have rightfully concluded that the ghosts in this book were the people we had never talked about, at least not at the depth they so richly deserved. What had been noted historically and anthropologically would never be enough for the record. The ghosts had become restless and could no longer be silenced.

In this book, I had tried to convince the reader that the pioneer culture which arose on the Great Plains after the Revolution set a standard to live by. They farmed, built schools, and established common laws to govern over local issues. Every Sunday they attended church and prayed for Heaven. Unfortunately, the Civil War fractured family stability setting kinfolk side by side and against each other. The war affected all people of color and culture. By account, there remained much we did not know about one another that needed to be heard.

What this book made me realize had been that our histories were being sold daily for profit. Internet blocks often kept me from accessing family records. I had to ask: as if to claim our lives for their safe keeping, who gave corporations the right to trade personal family documents and photographs while at the same time putting up walls of prohibition? In a very literal sense, technology had worked against me.

My parents had divorced when I was two years old so for the first fifty-two years of life, I knew very little about Riden inheritance. In retrospection, I would have liked to have known such things as a younger man. I became quite proud to have written this book without ever sourcing commercial outfits packaging most of my family history

Had I not become the watchman of my family in writing this book? Had I not reinvented myself as Bernardo in *Hamlet* urging Horatio to stand watch with him so that he may also see the apparition of the dead king? My kings were mortally departed, some erased gruesomely, but I admired them just the same.

The ghost of Uncle Fil Hancock allowed me to review the strange war phenomenon of safe-keeping one's enslaving captor. In Missouri, slaves protected their masters during the Civil War. Interestingly, Uncle Fil went down in history for being 'the witness' who saw General Lyon alive and then deceased. In Uncle Fil's domain at the time, a person may have thought that the unrest which descended upon Missouri in 1861 would have delivered some sense of encouragement to those enslaved but the counter effect occurred where children like Uncle Fil became terrified of federal soldiers. In the end, Uncle Fil became a hero of human beings.

The ghosts of Privates Leonard Garrett and John Leonard, both veterans of Valley Forge, made me feel confident that I had inherited the strength to move mountains. Tapping into these assets created a surmountable challenge. Having served the full term of their three-year enlistments, the Garrett's never deserted during the Revolution even when the chips were stacked against them. Grit, determination, and willpower became traits that Leonard and John Garrett transcended into successive generations. I knew this to be true because the earliest paper records in Arkansas and Missouri pioneer towns had Garrett and Riden fingerprints all over them.

The marriage of Miss Garrett and Riden Sr. stimulated searches on naming within Riden lines of descent that held a special and significant feature of the family; that being the first and middle name, Joseph Warren. It seemed easy to relate hero Dr. Joseph Warren killed at Breed's Hill with reasons why the Riden's used the names a lot, however, at the end of the discussion, it had been revealed that the habit of using Joseph Warren indeed originated from the American Revolution but probably at Valley Forge where several soldiers carried the Warren surname.

I remained questionable on how Elizabeth would have met Riden Sr.? It seemed possible that Private Leonard Garrett may have known Riden's father, Private James Riden III who had also served in the Revolution. Both men served in the infantry but not in the same unit. As for Dr. Warren, his bravery and sacrifice in the Revolution had been duly noted.

Of Elizabeth and Joseph Sr.'s children, none became more prominent in the Rolla and Duke community than Captain William Charles Riden. The flag I found on his grave two years ago showed that his accomplishments had not been forgotten. Obviously, my Cherokee cousins still remembered him with quiet honor and he remained on the Missouri Guard mailing list.

William Charles' second wife, Delilah Adeline Giddens, a Cherokee, became my step- grandmother in 1855. My blood grandmother Mary Huff Riden had died three years earlier. Interestingly, Grandmother Huff Riden looked to be 12 degrees away from one of George Washington sister's and 28 degrees away from Jean Baptiste Vimeur de Rochambeau. In both trees could be found the Garrett and Dent family connection. Nancy Garrett Dent and Elizabeth Garrett Riden showed up as significant ghosts in the lineage.

I had added three Hatley ghosts into the fray. Unlike the Riden's, my Hatley ancestors served with the Union as dragoons thus explaining to a degree why Grandfather Sam Hatley loved horses. Riding with the Ninth Kansas, Great Grandfather Leroy

Hatley had battled against units of Cherokee fighters led by the Adair's, a family that would later become some of the Hatley kinfolks' best friends. Leroy Hatley rode the same Eastern Oklahoma hills during his military service that Sam and Alma Hatley would one day call home.

Growing up in the summers with maternal grandmother Alma Collins Hatley of Stilwell, Oklahoma, I lived a life separated from my Indian heritage. I had played in the Oak Grove Cemetery in the old Goingsnake District absent from the realization of my own pedigree.

Grandma Hatley had a daughter who married a Walkingstick so my cousins inherited Cherokee genes but I did not see myself as anything but white. That changed three years ago when I learned of Susannah Stolen Horse and Hazel Bronaugh, names presented in my family tree with Cherokee and Choctaw-Cherokee underpinnings.

I honestly discovered the Oak Grove Cemetery spirit-filled with the Adair's as its first overseer. I viewed many Cherokee soldiers from America's wars buried in Oak Grove, their graves significantly weathered away by erosion. Cherokee slaves had also been entombed in the cemetery but without identification, meaning they had no headstones. According to Jess Adair, this seemed to be the prevailing secret about Oak Grove. Jess revealed the location to me shortly before his death.

Cherokee struggles in the Nation were unique in that the citizenry fought a civil war within a Civil War, dominantly over full and mixed bloodlines and the signers of treaties. The Treaty of New Echota divided the Nation and forever changed its history. Federal lies and deceit caused many Cherokee to side with the Confederacy during the Civil War and how could one blame them? George Adair and Balentine Adair served with distinction in the Confederate cause, survived and found their way back home to the beautiful foothills of the Ozarks, Stilwell, Oklahoma.

Preacher and Cherokee Principal Chief Downing became a double-dipper, having served for both sides during the conflict of 1861. He represented the difficult choice citizens had to make when war descended upon the sedentary people living in Indian Territory. For me, the chief represented strength during a time of horrific chaos. An enemy of Stand Watie, Chief Downing temporarily led the Nation after the death of Chief John Ross in 1866 and then later as its supreme authority. Over a 15-year career, he became the peacemaker of the Cherokee much like Chief Black Kettle of the Southern Cheyenne. Unfortunately, Chief Downing passed away from pneumonia in early winter, 1872. He never lived to see the land runs to come.

The Collins families seemed to mirror Chief Downing because many served on both sides of the Civil War. My take-away from Sergeant Collins could be summed up in a few ways: while I could never track the gene path of Sergeant Collins, I'm confident I mulled over cousins. There stood a high probability that Collins fought at Vicksburg, a siege in which more than 50 soldiers named Collins turned up as POWs. And yet, a big question remained unsolved: why was a grossly injured Confederate soldier and non-commissioned officer suffering from severe gangrene being held in a Confederate Prison?

My work into the Collins' revealed the fact that the families grew culturally diverse. With originations in Scotland and Ireland, to include the language of the Celtics, it wasn't surprising to find that the Collins' had African roots and this showed out in the USCT regiments. Because war had a tendency to force a collision of culture, if you will, then one could contrive with a degree of validity that the Collins' in Missouri grew from this intersection.

When I had landed in Duke, Missouri I'm not sure I actually realized it. I expected to find a small community named after a Confederate Officer, Basil Duke, but soon learned that the lawyer-officer had nothing to do with its name. I admired Basil because he practiced studying written law, which is something that had failed Captain Wesley Riden and his children in 1864. Basil's career started in Missouri when he served in the militia as a young captain.

It may have been a stretch to imply Basil Duke knew Captain Wesley Riden. In the *Rules of Combat They Never Taught You*, *Rule 11* addressed the fact that "if you are short of everything except the enemy, you are in combat" (U.S. Marine Corps Recruiting Page, 1992), a tenet Wesley had forgotten as a soldier, after all 'he's only walking down a road' with one of his twin newborns in his arms. I knew one thing to be absolutely finite about his death: "If the enemy is in range, so are you" (USMCRP, *Rule 16*, 1992).

I had looked at motive and intent as a legal angle on the Riden killings but in Missouri during the Civil War, everything seemed to have unraveled rather quickly in 1861. To be perfectly blunt, based on all the bushwhacking and murder that ensued, it appeared difficult to distinguish who was actually in charge of anything. What I could recall with specificity: my great uncle and cousins died painfully. Nothing could be more horrible than infant death.

There existed two opposed theories on the killings: Firstly, the Riden's had been in the right place at the wrong time if they were killed by happenstance means. Or secondly, Captain Riden had been purposely sought-out after being arrested twice by the law in Rolla. When the eyewitnesses stated that soldiers carried on the mayhem, that seemed to take the Provost out of the equation. I had initially considered a "hit" on Captain Riden by Hickok and the Provost Marshall's Office. However, children had been killed and therefore, I could not envision the law killing children nor could I accept the notion that lawmen hauled cannon?

Cannon, as told by eyewitnesses, had been used to kill Captain Riden and at least one child. I found what I believed to be the murder weapon at the Pea Ridge National Military Park, a Model 1841 12-pound Mountain Howitzer with unique features which could be pulled by a single horse. It's display showed that "four of these guns were used by Bowen's Missouri Cavalry

Battalion" and deployed "against Confederate ranks" (Pea Ridge NMP, March 23, 2018).

I had come across Colonel Bowen and studied him. He had killed a fellow senior Union officer which said something profoundly about his character. I alleged that Bowen fit into a larger puzzle regarding the Riden's. On the murder of the children, I believed the testimony that in fact both babies, Sarah and James Madison Riden, had died on the same day as their father.

There seemed to be no doubt that the murders had been committed by more than one person so Bowen couldn't have done it by himself. After all, Bowen commanded a battalion. In the end, I supported the theory that men from Bowen's battalion who had served with the colonel in the Battle of Elkhorn Tavern (See IMG8) murdered the Riden's because they would have had access to a mountain howitzer and known the Big Piney Area. I could not state that Bowen took part in the event, but he held an officer's responsibility to the matter.

Choice always seemed to have some measurable effect on who we became in the game of life. I would directly have agreed that there existed ghosts in my genes. But on the eighth day, the ghosts became silent and drifted from my perception. I could no longer hear their drum beats of war. They had passed through my memory like the wind rushing to master a new day. I settled for decoration instead.

With my mother, I visited the aging Cherokee plots in the Oak Grove Cemetery on a beautiful Sunday in May 2018 and then again in March 2021. I had finished where I had started: in a graveyard filled with ghosts of war. While propped up next to a large tomb of Civil War soldiers, I gazed at the query of clouds above my head and realized that in time I too would welcome death as a friend.

U.S. National Park Service, Department of the Interior

C.N.	Rank, Last Name, Initials	Unit, Company, Affiliation	
1.	Pvt. Riden, W.H.	2nd Regiment, SC. Infantry, Hotel Company	CSA
2.	Pvt. Riden, J.T.M.	8th Regiment, GA. Infantry, Echo Company	CSA
3.	Pvt. Riden, J.T.	Gartrell's Co., GA. Cavalry, Gartrell Company	CSA
4.	Pvt. Riden, Geo. W.	24th Regiment, GA. Infantry, Delta Company	CSA
5.	Pvt. Riden, William C.	24th Regiment, GA. Infantry, Delta Company	CSA
6.	Pvt. Riden, Josephus	34th Regiment, GA. Infantry, Echo Company	CSA
7.	Pvt. Riden, David	43rd Regiment, GA. Infantry, India Company	CSA
8.	Pvt. Riden, Mastin W.	Cobb's Legion, GA. Forces, Cobb	CSA
9.	Pvt. Riden, B.F.	38th Regiment, TN. Infantry, Foxtrot (Looney)	CSA
10.	Pvt. Riden, H.P.	38th Regiment, TN. Infantry, Foxtrot (Looney)	CSA
11.	Pvt. Riden, Geo. W.	50th Regiment, MO Infantry, Hotel Company	USA
12.	Cpl. Riden, Lorellen B.	26th Regiment, KY Infantry, Foxtrot/Bravo Co.	USA
13.	Sgt. Riden, John W.	26th Regiment, ILL. Infantry, USCT/Echo/C Co.	USA
14.	Cpl. Riden, John R.	2nd Regiment, TN. Cavalry, Bravo Company	USA
15.	Pvt. Riden, John W.	205th Regiment, PA. Infantry, Foxtrot Company	USA
16.	Pvt. Riden, German	102nd Regiment, PA. Infantry, Lima Company	USA
17.	Pvt. Riden, William	102nd Regiment, PA. Infantry, Lima Company	USA
18.	Pvt. Riden, John W.	131st Regiment, PA. Infantry, Delta Company	USA
19.	Pvt. Riden, Augustus	131st Regiment, PA. Infantry, Kilo Company	USA
20.	Sgt. Riden, Gustin R.	195th Regiment, PA. Infantry, Hotel Company	USA
21.	Pvt. Riden, Uriah K.	20th Regiment, PA. Cavalry, Echo Company	USA
22.	Pvt. Riden, Willis	20th Regiment, PA. Cavalry, Echo Company	USA
23.	Pvt. Riden, Robert I.	46th Regiment, PA. Infantry, Alpha Company	USA
24.	Cpl. Riden, James	49th Regiment, PA. Infantry, Hotel/Alpha Co.	USA
25.	Cpl. Riden, Gustin P.	78th Regiment, PA. Infantry, Charlie Company	USA
26.	Pvt. Riden, Lewis H.	78th Regiment, PA. Infantry, Charlie Company	USA
27.	Pvt. Riden, Samuel M.	78th Regiment, PA. Infantry, Kilo Company	USA
28.	Pvt. Riden, William C.	78th Regiment, PA Infantry, Charlie Company	USA

APPENDIX B

Primas Interview
June 24, 2016

Overview:

In 2016, during an expedition deep into the woodlands near Ft. Leonard Wood, I met with Professor Terry Primas of Duke, Missouri who was inimitably familiar with Pulaski County. Unplanned, I had stumbled on the gentleman looking for one of my lost Riden relatives while working a tip that I had received at the Licking Newspaper Office. Ironically, in Licking I met a long distance cousin by the name of Marie Lasater who had authored a book on the Riden's which featured a segment on the family cave. Before meeting the professor, I had read about Riden's Cave in a Guttenberg presentation.

Professor Primas worked at the antebellum house museum in Waynesville called the Old Stage Coach Stop. Primas edited the *Old Settlers Gazette Newspaper*. At one time, the professor had taken a crew of students to clean up the Warren-McCortney Cemetery on the Big Piney River. Though unknown to me at the time, it had been his article that I had initially stumbled across three years ago.

Our discussion centered on the cemetery and any scuttlebutt concerning my great uncle's death. Additionally, I needed to verify information about his children's deaths. The following annotations were taken from my notes in the interview:

Question 1: Do you think that Wesley Riden had been killed in the same battle at the McCortney Timber Mill with McCortney? His death is listed as March 1, 1864. This would not explain why the infants were killed on the same day.

Answer: The dates for Wesley Riden's death and the skirmish at McCortney's Mill do not coincide. The skirmish was on January 18, 1865. I checked the dates of other area skirmishes and none were on March 1, 1864.

Question 2: Sources indicated that Wesley Riden and the children were killed near McCourtney Hollow. Related to geography, where is McCortney Hollow located and how close is it to the mill?

Answer: Attached is a topographic map of this area. McCortney Hollow is a very long valley beginning on the west (left center) of the map. It extends eastward and the mouth is at the Big Piney River. Where you see Miller Spring is where the McCortney Mill was, with a short spring branch running to the river. McCortney Cemetery is across the river. I have placed an X where the cemetery is located right where the cross lines   intersect. I have placed a check mark where our house is to give you some sense of where things are. In the bottom right is the location of Riden's Cave. Hope this helps with the geography.

Question 3: Don't we have to have a skeleton to prove where someone is buried?

Answer: Usually a carved stone and/or record will suffice.

Question 4: Is it possible for me to visit the cave of my family?

Answer: Not at this time due to the bat population living in the cave.

The Rolla Fourteen
Missouri's Union Provost Marshal's Papers: 1861-1866

C.N.	Name	Rank, Affiliation	Comments
1.	Wesley Riden	Captain, C.S.A.	Killed by Union Soldiers in 1864
2.	George H. Hume	Captain, C.S.A.	2nd Mo. Regt. Survived the war
3.	David Crossland	Private, Union	63rd Regt MM. Enrolled in 1864
4.	Robert H. Barker	Private, Union	McNutt's Co. Enrolled in 1864
5.	Levi Scott	Private, C.S.A.	10th Mo. Regt. Deserted Nov. 1862
6.	James Helm	Private, C.S.A.	KIA, 1862, Battle of Lone Jack
6.	James Helm	2nd Lt., Union	13th Cavalry Regt. Joined Rolla 1864
6.	James Helm	Private, Union	10th Cavalry Regt. Joined Sept 1862
7.	F.M. Welsh	Private, Union	49th Infantry Regt. Survived the war
8.	Richard Martin	7 Name Matches	Unclear and Not Identified
9.	William Adams	Private, C.S.A.	KIA, 1864, Battle of Jenkins Ferry
10.	John Helm	8 Name Matches	Unclear and Not Identified
11.	J. Stone	19 Name Matches	Unclear and Not Identified
12.	M. Stone	Private, Union	66th Regt. MM. Enrolled in 1862
12.	M. Stone	Corporal, Union	47th Infantry Regt. Survived the war
13.	M. Courtney	Private, C.S.A.	Shanks' Regt. Survived the war
14.	H. Tompkins	3 Name Matches	Unclear and Not Identified

George "Shack" Washington: The Fifteenth Ghost

I had a life-changing memory of the fifteenth ghost. For years, I supposed that mother worried about my first taste of manhood. One night deep in the Alabama woods, the ghost showed me how to relieve an injured animal from its misery. God knows I was only about six years old at the time and barely a graduate of first grade. I learned at a young age the definitive line between life and death.

The ghost of George "Shack" Washington (1911-1997) lived in Frankville, Alabama with the county bearing the first president's name. His ancestors may have been slaves on the Washington Plantation of Virginia. While our time together proved brief, Shack's influence in my life would become something I would not discover until adulthood.

I met Shack in 1967 through my mother's fiancé, Audrey. As his name implied, Shack lived on a dirt road in a dilapidated wood shack in an open field with a pond in front of the house and to its side. An older man, probably nearing 60 years, Shack would end up protecting me when our raccoon hunting party had been halted by the grunting of several wild boars that we could not see. Shack carried me across a river in complete darkness. In 1992, Jim Haskins had written *One More River to Cross* which highlighted Black Americans. I connected spiritually and immediately.

Audrey's family had hunted raccoons at night for years, but I don't remember being interested in eating or killing them. One of the dogs had chased a raccoon up a tree and the men had shot it down to the ground but it was still alive. I was then asked to fire one round into the raccoon's brain. While Shack held my hand, using his pistol, I fired thus relieving the poor animal from its suffering.

I'm not sure I ever feared weapons after the event but I did gain a valuable respect for things that were dangerous and could kill. Sadly, I never saw Shack again but believe still today that my time with him came from the order of angels. From Shack, I learned that 'sometimes men had to do things they normally wouldn't do.' More than this, I formed a life-lasting love affair for people of color and culture.

REFERENCE

Anderson, E. Mc D. (1868). *Memoirs: Historical and personal,including the campaigns of the   First Missouri Confederate Brigade*. St. Louis, MO: Times Print Company Street.

Anderson, W.L. (2009). Ross, William Potter. *The Encyclopedia of Oklahoma History and   Culture*. Retrieved from http://www.okhistory.org/publications/enc/entry.php?entry=R O032

Archives of Maryland Online. *Maryland State Archives*. Retrieved from http://aomol.msa.maryland.gov/html/index.html

Barr, A. E. (1836). The farmer. *Literature Network*. Retrieved from http://www.online-literature.com/amelia-barr/4386/

Brooks, R.B. (2013). William Quantrill's three graves. *Civil War Saga*. Retrieved from http://civilwarsaga.com/william-quantrills-three-graves/ **Bryan**, W.S. & Rose, R. (1876). *A history of the pioneer families of Missouri: Toronto Collection*. St. Louis, MO: Bryan Brand & Company.   **Cassidy**, J.J., Walker, B., Cressy, J., DiBerardino, L., Lawrynenko, L., Sculco, G., ...Silver, Y. Eds.   (1995). *Through Indian eyes: The untold story of Native American Peoples*. Pleasantville,   NY: Readers Digest Association.   **Cherokee Registry**.com (2015). Cherokee Heritage Documentation Center: Stand Watie-list of   soldiers who served. Retrieved from http://cherokeeregistry.com/ index.php?option= com_content&view=article&id= 396&Itemid=594

Chesapeake Illustrated (2010). *Quote of the day, volume IV*. Oklahoma City, Ok: Chesapeake   Energy. **Civil War Soldiers** (2015). William Hatley: Private of the Union Army. Retrieved on Jan 31, 2015 from http://civil-war-soldiers.findthebest.com/l/2407208/William-Hatley **Civil War Index** – Gettysburg Campaign. Series I. Volume XXVII. Part III.   Retrieved on July 17,   2015 from http://www.civilwar.com/?option=com_officialrecord&series=S eries %20I&volume =Volume%20XXVII&part=Part%20III&page=728

Civil War Index – Little Rock. Series I. Volume XXII. Part II. 758. Retrieved on July 17, 2015 from http://civilwar.com/components/index.php?option=com_officialrecord&series=Series%20I&volume=Volume%20XXII&part=Part%20II&page=758

Civil War Trust (2017). Biography: John C. Pemberton. Retrieved on July 6, 2017 from https://www.civilwar.org/learn/biographies/john-c-pemberton

Civil War Trust (2018). History of the Cherokees at Pea Ridge. Retrieved on February 4, 2018 from https://www.civilwar.org/learn/articles/cherokees-pea-ridge

Community and Conflict, 3437: The Impact of the Civil War in the Ozarks. Coleman Bruce Papers. Retrieved on July 21, 2015 from http://www.ozarkscivilwar.org/archives/3437

Community and Conflict, 585: The Impact of the Civil War in the Ozarks. James "Wild Bill" Hickok. Retrieved on July 22, 2015 from http://www.ozarkscivilwar.org/archives/585

Connelley, W. (1956). My Dear Mother. In Q*uantrill and the Border Wars*. Pageant Book Co.

Cook, Walter W. (1917). Act, intention, and motive in criminal law. In Lord C.J. Kenyon, the   intent and the act must concur to constitute the crime: Fowler v. Padget (1798). *Yale Law Journal, 26*(8), 645-663.

Cornell University & United States War Department (1902). The War of the Rebellion: A Compilation of the Official Records of the Union and Confederate Armies, Series 1, Volume 22 Part I. Retrieved May 1, 2015 from http://ebooks.library.cornell.edu

Davis, W.C. (1999). *Portraits of the Civil War*. New York, NY: Smithmark Publishers.

Davis, W.C. (1981). *Battle at Bull Run: A history of the first major campaign of the Civil War*.   LSU Press.

De Jean, T. (2012). Burial Traditions in the Region of the Upper Cumberland Plateau.   Retrieved from http://www.nps.gov/biso/historyculture/upload/FINALburialTR ADS.pdf

Divine, R.A., Breen, T.H., Fredrickson, G.M., Williams, R.H., Gross, A.J., & Brands, H.W. (2007).   *The American story, volume I to 1877, third edition*. New York, NY: Pearson Education.

Dyer, F.H. (1908). *A compendium of the war of the rebellion*. Des Moines, IA: Dyer Publishing. **Dylan,** B. (1967). "All along the watchtower." John Wesley Harding Album. Produced by Bob Johnston. Columbia Records.

Eliot, T.S. (1925). The Hollow Men. Retrieved from Michigan State University at https://msu.edu/~jungahre/transmedia/the-hollow-men.html

Erwin, J.W. (2013). *Guerilla hunters in Civil War Missouri*. Charleston, SC: History Press.

Erwin, J.W. (2012). *Guerillas in Civil War Missouri*. Charleston, SC: History Press.

Filby & Meyer (1985). A guide to published arrival records of about 500, 000 passengers who   came to the United States and Canada in the 17th, 18th, and 19th centuries.

Find a Grave.com (2015a). John Garrett Grave. Retrieved from http://www.findagrave.com/cgi-bin/fg.cgi?page=gr&GSln=Garrett&GSfn=John +&GSbyrel=all&GSdyrel=all&GSob=n&GSsr= 41&GRid=6951625&df=all&

Find a Grave.com (2015b). William Charles Riden Grave. Retrieved from http://www.findagrave.com/cgi-bin/fg.cgi?page=gr&GSln=Riden&GSiman=1&GScid= 27510&GRid=11377478&

Flanders, L.B. (1836). A Departed Brother. Appeared in the *New York Mercury Newspaper*.   Retrieved from http://ozarkscivilwar.org/photographs/fine-flavius-j/

Foner, E. (2006). Give me liberty! An American history, volume I. NY: W.W. Norton & Company

Ford Jr., L.K. (1988). *Origins of southern radicalism: The South Carolina upcountry, 1800-1860*.   New York, NY: Oxford University Press.

Fowke, G. (2006). Archaeological Investigations: Bureau of American Ethnology, Bulletin 76.   Retrieved on January 17, 2016 from http://www.gutenberg.org/files/18931/18931- h/18931-h.htm

Franks, K.A. (2009). Watie, Stand. *The Encyclopedia of Oklahoma History and Culture.* Retrieved from http://www.okhistory.org/publications/enc/entry.php?entry=W A040

Gaines, W.C. (1989). *The Confederate Cherokees: John Drew's regiment of mounted rifles*. Baton Rouge, LA: Louisiana State University Press.

Goodspeed Document (1888). History of Franklin, Jefferson, Washington, Crawford, and   Gasconade counties Missouri. p. 254. Retrieved from http://home.usmo.com/~momollus/FranCoCW/BowenMOReg. htm

Goodspeed Document (1889). County records of Texas County Missouri, military troops and   taxpayer List. Retrieved from http://texas.mogenweb.org/goodspeed/taxpayers.htm

Goodspeed Document (1971). History of Laclede, Camden, Dallas, Webster, Wright, Texas,   Pulaski, Phelps, and Dent Counties. In *Community and Conflict*. Chicago, Illinois: Goodspeed   Publishing.

Hatley, James. Letter to Alma Hatley dated January 24, 2007. Family archives.

Haywood, J. (1995). *The penguin historical atlas of the Vikings*. London: Penguin Group.

Henderson, P. & Ancestory.com Roots Web (2004). Garrett-L Archives. Retrieved from http://archiver.rootsweb.ancestry.com/th/read/GARRETT/2004-03/1078673412

Henderson, L. (1960). *Roster of the Confederate Soldiers of Georgia 1861-1865*. From the Georgia State Division of   Confederate Prisons and Records. Longina & Porter 1959.

Higginson, Col. T.W., & Gray, G.S. (1970). Army life in a black regiment: The adventures of the   First South Carolina Volunteers. Grosset & Dunlap: New York.

Hosmer, W.H.C. (1873). Later lays and lyrics. Rochester, NY: D.M. Dewey.

Hoy, K.M. (2017, No. 2445). Biography of Wesley Garrett. Retrieved on March 23, 2018 from https://www.wikitree.com/wiki/Garrett-2445

Hoy, K.M. (2017, No. 37). Biography of William Charles Riden. Retrieved on March 23, 2018 from https://www.wikitree.com/wiki/Riden-37 **Kansas Adjutant General's Office** (1867). *Report of the adjutant general of the State of Kansas, volume 1, 1861-1865*. Chicago, IL: Bulletin Co-operative Printing Company.

Kensey, P. (2002). West Point Classmates-Civil War Enemies. Retrieved from http://www.american civilwar.asn.au/meet/2002_10_mtg_westpt_classmates_enemies.pdf

Lundberg Nee Sternburg, TS (2010). G.W. Adair & Confederate regular troops. Retrieved from https://www.findagrave.com/cgi-bin/fg.cgi?page=mr&MRid=46889000

Maryland State Archives (2018). Muster rolls and other records of service of Maryland troops in the American Revolution, volume 18, p. 687. *Archives of Maryland Online*. Retrieved from http://msa.maryland.gov/megafile/msa/speccol/sc2900/sc2908/000001

Missouri Gravestones Project, No. 810327 (2018). Sarah Amanda Richards Hatley. Retrieved on March 27, 2018 from https://missourigravestones.org/view.php?id=810327

Missouri History Museum (2009). Civil War Collections. Medical Certificate of W.H. Collins August 10, 1864. Retrieved on May 8, 2016 from http://cdm.sos.mo.gov/cdm/ref/collection/CivilWar/id/15636

Missouri's Union Provost Marshal's Papers: 1861-1866. Retrieved on February 12, 2015 from http://www.sos.mo.gov/archives/provost/results.asp?txtKeyword=&radSearch=BEG&selCounty=Phelps&offset=675

mocivilwar.org (2015). Missouri's Civil War Heritage. Basil, Duke. Retrieved on April 17, 2015 and July 8, 2017 from http://mocivilwar.org/portfolio/basil-duke/

Morrison, J. (1979). An American Prayer. Produced by J. Haeny, R. Manzarek, R. Krieger, J. Densmore, & F. Lisciandro. Elektra/Asylum Records.

Moser Report (Year Unknown). A Directory of Towns, Villages, and Hamlets Past and Present of Phelps County, Missouri. Retrieved from https://thelibrary.org/lochist/moser/phelpspl.html

murraycountymuseum.com (2017). Civil War for Murray and surrounding counties. Company A 39th Regiment, Murray County Cohutta Rangers. Retrieved on July 7, 2017 from http://murraycountymuseum.com/cwr_06.html

National Institute for Genealogy Studies – Genealogy Wise (2015). Public Member Story by M. Martin on the Death of Captain

John Wesley Riden. Retrieved on May 23, 2015 from http://www. genealogywise.com/ group/lookupvolunteers/forum/topics/need-   ancestry-look-up?xg_source=activity

New York State Military Museum and Veterans Research Center (2015). Rosters of the NY   Infantry Regiments during the Civil War. Retrieved from http://dmna.ny.gov/historic /reghist/civil/rosters/rostersinfantry.htm

Ohio State University (2018, 1895). War of Rebellion: Serial 003, Operations in Missouri, Arkansas, Kansas, and Indian Territory, Chapter X. Retrieved from http://ehistory. osu.edu/books/official-records/003

Osage County.org & Cornell University Library (2015). Civil War Records for Gasconade, Maries, and Osage Counties: Extract   from The War of the Rebellion: a Compilation of the   Official Records of the Union and Confederate Armies. Retrieved from http://www.osagecounty.org/civilwar/cw-index.html

Owen, W. (1917). The Unreturning. The Wilfred Owen Association. Retrieved from http://www.wilfredowen.org.uk/poetry/the-unreturning

Parrish, W.E. (1965). *Missouri under radical rule, 1865-1870*. Columbia: University of Missouri   Press.

Pink Floyd (1979). The Trial. The Wall Album. Produced by B. Ezrin, D. Gilmour, J. Guthrie & R. Waters. Harvest/Columbia Records.

Powell, W.S. Ed. (2006). *Encyclopedia of North Carolina*. Chapel Hill, NC: University of North   Carolina Press.

Report of the Adjutant General of the State of Kansas, Volume 1 - 1861-1865. Leavenworth,   Kansas: Bulletin Co-operative Printing Company. Chicago. 1867. Retrieved on May 1,   2016 from http://www.ksgenweb.com/ archives/statewide/military/civilwar   /adjutant/index2.html

Ruchti, S.J. (2016, Abstract). The mass of men lead lives of quiet desperation: A study of unconventional point of view and narrative structures in contemporary fiction. Conference on Undergraduate Research, University of Montana.

Stacey, A.L.D. (1890s ca.). Unidentified man. Missouri Valley Special Collections, Kansas City Public Library DVD98: MVO-85F. [Photograph] Retrieved on January 15, 2018 at http://www.kchistory.org/content/unidentified-man

State Historical Society of Missouri-Civil War Manuscripts & Western Historical Manuscript Collection 1885. Allen, Wellington Reminiscence (C0692). Retrieved from http://cdm16795. contentdm.oclc.org/cdm/compoundobject/collection/ whmccivwar/id/26/rec/1

Stewart, R.W. Ed. (2008). American Military History, Volume I: The United States Army and the Forging of a Nation, 1775-1917. *United States Army Center of Military History.* Washington, DC: CMH Pub 30-21.

Sturm, C.D. (2002). *Blood politics: Race, culture, and identity in the Cherokee Nation of Oklahoma.* Oakland, CA: University of California Press.

Taney Project (2015). Alf Bolin. The Terror of the Hills. In *Taney and Beyond: A Regional Studies Forum for Teachers and Students.* Retrieved on June 27, 2015 from http://www.projecttaney.org/alfbolin.html

Thoborn (1924). The Cherokee Question. *Chronicles of Oklahoma, volume 2, no. 2,* June, 1924. Retrieved from http://digital.library.okstate.edu/chronicles/v002/v002p141.ht ml

U.S. Government War Archives. Phelps County Burials. Retrieved on July 4, 2016 from http://www.usgwarchives.net/mo/phelps/burials/phelps_burial s_401.htm

U.S. Marine Corps Recruiting Page, 1992. Xerox Copy of "Rules of
Combat They Never Taught   You." Rule 11; 1-20.

U.S. National Park Service. Department of the Interior. Soldiers and
Sailors Data Base: Civil   War. Retrieved on June 17, 2016 from
http://www.nps.gov/civilwar/soldiers-and-sailors-database.htm

Walsh, J. (1985). The Confessor. From the Album by the same name.
Produced by J. Walsh and K. Olsen. Full Moon Records.

Wildrick, G.C. (2009). Dr. Joseph Warren: Leader in Medicine, Politics,
and Revolution. *Baylor   University Medical Center, National
Institutes of Health, 22*(1), 27-29.

2ndMissouri.com (2015). 2nd Missouri Infantry: History of the 2nd
Missouri. Retrieved at
http://www.2ndmissouri.com/historyofthe2ndmissouri

--END--

www.ingramcontent.com/pod-product-compliance
Lightning Source LLC
Chambersburg PA
CBHW071358120626
46546CB00002B/739